CAMBRIDGE
UNIVERSITY PRESS

CAMBRIDGE ENGLISH
Language Assessment
Part of the University of Cambridge

Cambridge English

CAMBRIDGE OFFICIAL PREPARATION MATERIAL

FIRST for Schools 3

WITH ANSWERS

AUTHENTIC EXAMINATION PAPERS

Cambridge University Press
www.cambridge.org/elt

Cambridge Assessment English
www.cambridgeenglish.org

Information on this title: www.cambridge.org/9781108433785

First published 2018

20 19 18 17 16 15 14 13 12 11 10 9 8 7 6 5 4 3 2

Printed in Great Britain by CPI Group (UK) Ltd, Croydon CRO 4YY

A catalogue record for this publication is available from the British Library

ISBN 978-1-108-43378-5 Student's Book with answers
ISBN 978-1-108-38085-0 Student's Book with answers with Audio
ISBN 978-1-108-43376-1 Student's Book without answers
ISBN 978-1-108-43381-5 Audio CDs (2)

Contents

Introduction

This collection of four complete practice tests comprises papers from the *Cambridge English: First for Schools* examination; students can practise these tests on their own or with the help of a teacher.

The *Cambridge English: First for Schools* examination is part of a suite of general English examinations produced by Cambridge English Language Assessment. This suite consists of five examinations that have similar characteristics but are designed for different levels of English language ability. Within the five levels, *Cambridge English: First for Schools* is at Level B2 in the Council of Europe's *Common European Framework of Reference for Languages: Learning, teaching, assessment.* It has been accredited by Ofqual, the statutory regulatory authority in England, at Level 1 in the National Qualifications Framework. The *Cambridge English: First for Schools* examination is widely recognised in commerce and industry and in individual university faculties and other educational institutions.

Examination	Council of Europe Framework Level	UK National Qualifications Framework Level
Cambridge English: Proficiency *Certificate of Proficiency in English (CPE)*	C2	3
Cambridge English: Advanced *Certificate in Advanced English (CAE)*	C1	2
Cambridge English: First for Schools *First Certificate in English (FCE) for Schools*	B2	1
Cambridge English: Preliminary *Preliminary English Test (PET)*	B1	Entry 3
Cambridge English: Key *Key English Test (KET)*	A2	Entry 2

Cambridge English: First for Schools follows the same format as *Cambridge English: First* and the level of the question papers is identical. The only difference is that the content and treatment of topics in *Cambridge English: First for Schools* have been particularly targeted at the interest and experience of school pupils. *Cambridge English: First for Schools* candidates who achieve Grade C or higher in the exam receive a *Cambridge English: First for Schools* certificate.

Further information

The information contained in this practice book is designed to be an overview of the exam. For a full description of all of the above exams, including information about task types, testing focus and preparation, please see the relevant handbooks which can be obtained from Cambridge English Language Assessment at the address below or from the website at: www.cambridgeenglish.org

Cambridge English Language Assessment
1 Hills Road
Cambridge CB1 2EU
United Kingdom

Telephone: +44 1223 553997
Email: helpdesk@cambridgeenglish.org

The structure of *Cambridge English: First for Schools*: an overview

The *Cambridge English: First for Schools* examination consists of four papers.

Reading and Use of English 1 hour 15 minutes
This paper consists of **seven parts**, with 52 questions. For Parts 1 to 4, the test contains texts with accompanying grammar and vocabulary tasks, and separate items with a grammar and vocabulary focus. For Parts 5 to 7, the test contains a range of texts and accompanying reading comprehension tasks.

Writing 1 hour 20 minutes
This paper consists of **two parts** which carry equal marks. In Part 1, which is **compulsory**, candidates have to write an essay of between 140 and 190 words, giving their opinion in response to a task. In Part 2, there are four tasks from which candidates **choose one** to write about. The range of tasks from which questions may be drawn includes an article, an email/letter, an essay, a review and a short story. The last question is based on a set text. In this part, candidates have to write between 140 and 190 words.

Listening 40 minutes (approximately)
This paper consists of **four parts.** Each part contains a recorded text or texts and some questions, including multiple-choice, sentence completion and multiple-matching. Each text is heard twice. There is a total of **30 questions.**

Speaking 14 minutes
The Speaking test consists of **four parts.** The standard test format is two candidates and two examiners. One examiner takes part in the conversation while the other examiner listens. Both examiners give marks. Candidates will be given photographs and other visual and written materials to look at and talk about. Sometimes candidates will talk with the other candidate, sometimes with the examiner, and sometimes with both.

Grading

Candidates will receive a score on the Cambridge English Scale for each of the four skills and Use of English. The average of these five scores gives the candidate's overall Cambridge English Scale score for the exam. This determines what grade and CEFR level they achieve. All candidates receive a Statement of Results and candidates who pass the examination with Grade A, B or C also receive the *First Certificate in English*. Candidates who achieve Grade A receive the *First Certificate in English* stating that they demonstrated ability at Level C1. Candidates who achieve Grade B or C receive the *First Certificate in English* certificate stating that they demonstrated ability at Level B2. Candidates whose performance is below B2 level, but falls within Level B1, receive a *Cambridge English* certificate stating that they have demonstrated ability at Level B1. Candidates whose performance falls below Level B1 do not receive a certificate.

For further information on grading and results, go to the website (see page 5).

Test 1

READING AND USE OF ENGLISH (1 hour 15 minutes)

Part 1

For questions **1–8**, read the text below and decide which answer (**A**, **B**, **C** or **D**) best fits each gap. There is an example at the beginning (**0**).

Mark your answers **on the separate answer sheet.**

Example:

0 **A** describes **B** suggests **C** explains **D** shows

0	A	B	C	D
	▭	▬	▭	▭

Chocolate teapots really are useful

A chocolate teapot is not as useless as the old British saying **(0)** .... Scientists have shown it's possible to use one to make tea. They've created a chocolate teapot that can be filled with boiling water and left to **(1)** .... for two minutes, after which the tea is ready to be served.

After **(2)** .... a range of experiments, the scientists **(3)** .... to the conclusion that the **(4)** .... to making a teapot that wouldn't melt was to use dark chocolate with 65% chocolate solids and build up a series of layers to strengthen it. This whole process took around two-and-a-half hours.

At first the scientists wondered whether they might **(5)** .... end up with chocolate tea. They discovered some of the chocolate on the inside of the pot would melt, but **(6)** .... that the water was poured in carefully, the **(7)** .... majority of it wouldn't be affected. When they tried the tea, the team agreed it was lovely with a **(8)** .... taste of chocolate.

1	**A**	hold	**B**	keep	**C**	stand	**D**	wait
2	**A**	investigating	**B**	conducting	**C**	researching	**D**	exploring
3	**A**	arrived	**B**	reached	**C**	drew	**D**	came
4	**A**	secret	**B**	clue	**C**	method	**D**	formula
5	**A**	again	**B**	still	**C**	clearly	**D**	simply
6	**A**	allowed	**B**	considered	**C**	provided	**D**	assumed
7	**A**	huge	**B**	broad	**C**	high	**D**	vast
8	**A**	modest	**B**	slight	**C**	soft	**D**	gentle

Part 2

For questions **9–16**, read the text below and think of the word which best fits each gap. Use only **one** word in each gap. There is an example at the beginning (**0**).

Write your answers **IN CAPITAL LETTERS on the separate answer sheet.**

Example: | 0 | H A V E |

Making mistakes helps you to succeed

(0) .... you ever tried a new sport or learnt to play a musical instrument? **(9)** .... so, you'll know that once you figure **(10)** .... how to do it and get good at it, you won't lose your skills, even when you haven't practised for a long time. Most experts put this down to 'muscle memory', which means the brain remembers an action and can recall it when needed. Now some researchers believe there's another important factor: errors that occur while learning a task.

(11) .... surprised the researchers is that getting things wrong not only trains the brain to perform better at a specific task, but also helps it to learn faster. This is true even when mistakes are **(12)** .... while learning a completely new task. The researchers believe that the brain keeps a record **(13)** .... errors and draws on them whenever a new skill **(14)** .... being learnt. This ensures that mistakes aren't repeated, and probably explains why people **(15)** .... master one sport or instrument can pick **(16)** .... others with relative ease.

Part 3

For questions **17–24**, read the text below. Use the word given in capitals at the end of some of the lines to form a word that fits in the gap **in the same line**. There is an example at the beginning (**0**).

Write your answers **IN CAPITAL LETTERS on the separate answer sheet.**

Example: | **0** | A | M | A | Z | I | N | G |

Have a go at kayaking

I've discovered an **(0)** .... sport: kayaking. It looks very	**AMAZE**
(17) .... when you see it on TV, and apparently it's been increasing in	**IMPRESS**
(18) .... over the past few years. I'm not actually a very sporty	**POPULAR**
person but when my sister, a keen kayaker herself, bought me a lesson	
for my birthday that was my opportunity to have a go.	
It was a **(19)** .... to discover I wasn't the only beginner – everyone	**RELIEVE**
else was also very **(20)** .... like me. At first we were all pretty	**EXPERIENCE**
(21) .... and some of us even fell in the water, but we learnt quickly	**HOPE**
and our confidence began to grow.	
I loved being on the river. The **(22)** .... were so beautiful and	**SURROUND**
relaxing that I was really reluctant to get out of the kayak when	
the lesson finished! It was a truly **(23)** .... day. I signed up for a	**MEMORY**
one-week course without a moment's hesitation. Now I'm just as	
(24) .... about kayaking as my sister.	**PASSION**

Part 4

For questions **25–30**, complete the second sentence so that it has a similar meaning to the first sentence, using the word given. **Do not change the word given**. You must use between **two** and **fiv** words, including the word given. Here is an example (**0**).

Example:

0 Prizes are given out when the school year finishes.

PLACE

Prize-giving .... end of the school year.

The gap can be filled by the words 'takes place at the', so you write:

Example:	**0**	*TAKES PLACE AT THE*

Write **only** the missing words **IN CAPITAL LETTERS on the separate answer sheet.**

---

25 Seeing Pete sitting in the café was a real surprise.

EXPECTED

I really .... Pete sitting in the café.

26 My aunt said we could stay at her house for a few nights during the holidays.

PUT

My aunt said she could .... at her house for a few nights during the holidays.

27 Anne says she doesn't want to make the effort to tidy her room, even though it's a mess!

BOTHERED

Anne says she .... to tidy her room, even though it's a mess!

28 Could you look after my little brother for a minute, please?

EYE

Could you .... my little brother for a minute, please?

29 Jo's mother told her that it wasn't a good idea to eat so many biscuits before lunch!

DISCOURAGE

Jo's mother tried .... so many biscuits before lunch!

30 The teacher didn't think about the fact that it might rain when she planned the school trip.

ACCOUNT

The teacher failed .... the fact that it might rain when she planned the school trip.

Part 5

You are going to read an extract from an interview with a young novelist. For questions **31–36**, choose the answer (**A**, **B**, **C** or **D**) which you think fits best according to the text.

Mark your answers **on the separate answer sheet.**

Young writer

Charlotte Grainger explains that it was her primary school teacher who first speculated that she might write a novel. 'I thought the height of achievement would be to write a book because it seemed such a challenge and anyway I didn't know what other teenagers were doing, like being in the Olympics, for example. When I turned 13 I thought: "I may as well attempt this now".' The novel Charlotte started then is, remarkably, about to be published. 'Recently I told my ex-teacher about it and she was astonished. She told me she'd meant I'd probably do it when I was 30 or 40. That had never occurred to me – I couldn't understand why I'd be expected to put something on hold that I had a chance of being good at.'

It's a winter afternoon, in the offices of Charlotte's publishers. Even though I knew that I was going to interview a 15-year-old girl about her book, I was still momentarily thrown by seeing a teenager sitting there. The book is a huge achievement: the narrative is assured and action packed. Nothing about it, except the age of its heroine, suggests that it was written by a teenager. The public relations representative for the book is keeping us company in case Charlotte might need defending. But she needs neither parental nor professional support. She's her own person: spirited, with an alert face and a lively intelligence, but also a steadiness that prevents any overconfidence she could be forgiven for feeling.

I ask her about the sophisticated moral issues she raises. 'I was trying to ask big questions, not answer them. There aren't many life lessons I can pass on to my readers,' she responds, laughing. 'I don't think my understanding of the world is limited by my age, but neither do I believe I'm particularly wise. I was just interested in exploring the theme of taking responsibility.'

She has a theory about teenagers and the way they are 'betrayed' by the fiction that is specifically aimed at them. There are, she maintains, three types of teenager depicted in novels. 'There's the outsider who becomes acceptable to society, the naïve teenager who knows nothing about the big wide world, and the awkward teenage character who isn't socially skilled.' Repeatedly reading about these character types irritated her. 'What if you're basically fine? There aren't many stories out there about characters who aren't inadequate in some way. The overall impression teenagers can get from some writers – and I don't think it's intentional – is teenagers can't possibly know who they are because they're not experienced enough to know the truth. And when that *line 58*
is being pushed on them by writers, it can undermine their self-belief'.

Charlotte has always been a keen reader of famous fantasy writers, some of whom you might suppose she'd be indebted to, but in fact they almost put her off writing entirely. 'Books by my favourite fantasy writers explore deep things about psychology and about life. I was asking myself: is this seriously what I have to be doing to write a good book and am I really up to it?' She does, however, praise the influence of a book called *How Not to Write a Novel*. 'It tells you that if the reader starts to guess what's going to happen, the suspense has probably gone.'

It would be easy to argue that Charlotte's parents both being journalists was the decisive factor in getting her novel published. Indeed, her father's acquaintance with someone in publishing was what got her book read initially. She acknowledges her good fortune, because getting anyone to read a first novel is hard, whatever the age of the author. 'Every aspiring writer needs support and a lucky break, but after that you're on your own. Ultimately writers sink or swim according to their talents so I don't take things for granted,' Charlotte concludes.

31 Charlotte says she wrote her first novel when she was only 13 because

A she thought it was the easiest way to achieve something great.
B she found it impossible to imagine that delaying was an option.
C she was determined to prove that age was no barrier to success.
D she wanted to live up to her teacher's high expectations of her.

32 What does the writer say about Charlotte in the second paragraph?

A She should take more advice from others.
B She is more modest than might be expected.
C She is more confident in her abilities than she should be.
D She should be allowed more independence.

33 What does Charlotte feel about the characters in teenage fiction?

A They are people who lack confidence or self-awareness.
B They are people with qualities that aren't believable.
C They are created by writers with no interest in young people.
D They are people that readers can identify with easily.

34 What does 'that' refer to in line 58?

A a criticism of how teenagers behave
B the harsh reality of everyday life for teenagers
C an alternative viewpoint for teenagers to consider
D an assumption about the nature of teenagers

35 What was Charlotte's attitude to the famous writers she read?

A She was pleased that they dealt with topics she was interested in.
B She was disappointed by the predictable nature of some stories.
C She became aware of how challenging it would be to write in a similar way.
D She became conscious of the way they had stimulated her imagination.

36 How does she feel about her experience of writing?

A She is annoyed that people focus on how fortunate she has been.
B She regrets that she may have to depend on others.
C She accepts that her early success may not continue.
D She doubts that people fully appreciate her talent.

Part 6

You are going to read a newspaper article about research on the effect of light on students. Six sentences have been removed from the article. Choose from the sentences **A–G** the one which fits each gap (**37–42**). There is one extra sentence which you do not need to use.

Mark your answers **on the separate answer sheet.**

Lighting up the winter darkness

In northern Scandinavia the long dark winters can be difficult. The students in Dragonskolan, a secondary school in Umeå, in Sweden's far north, are taking part in an experiment to see whether using intense electric light, known as 'full-spectrum' light, can help with this problem. This light is much brighter than the lighting currently used in most schools and homes.

This experiment is also part of a bigger debate about using full-spectrum light in schools to relieve tiredness and lack of energy. These symptoms can develop when sleep patterns are disturbed by the very long nights. **37** It is not unusual, for example, for some students to fall asleep on the journey to school.

But last month Dragonskolan school installed 140 full-spectrum lamps in several classrooms. Now, stepping through the door in the morning is like walking into bright sunshine. Students even find themselves glancing out of the window, surprised to see that the sun hasn't come up yet. **38**

The school is the first to use this simple technique to try to improve students' performance. Light tells the brain to halt production of melatonin – the hormone that makes you sleepy. **39** Researcher Dr Mariana Figueiro believes that, during the winter, the effects of the lack of light can slowly build up and make your 'body clock' confused. Exposure to light of the correct wavelength and intensity helps the body to know when to switch off in the evening. So you sleep more and feel better the next morning.

40 When a sleep researcher at Stockholm told a conference of head teachers about the benefits of installing full-spectrum lights, they objected, saying that pupils would become restless and be unable to concentrate on their work. Money was also a concern for them because some schools didn't have the budget for these lights.

But those like Figueiro, who are arguing for change, point to other evidence to support their case. **41** Designers may have ignored the significance of this, as giving any consideration to light in their designs seems to have become too low a priority.

For all these reasons, it's not surprising that only a few head teachers have experimented with the lighting in their schools. At Dragonskolan, head teacher Stellan Andersson initially understood this reluctance. After all, some studies suggested that although people claimed the brighter lights were having a positive effect on them, there was no measurable evidence to support this. Equally though, there was no evidence that they actually caused any harm. **42** So Andersson decided to go ahead with installing them hoping for better academic performance. But, whether this happens or not, the students are certainly enjoying the bright new teaching environment.

A Without that stimulus, the body delays, by a few minutes every day, the signal that it's time to wake up.

B What's more, it seems that sitting in a brightly lit room could help people cope with this.

C In fact, there's a much more positive atmosphere there these days.

D Light was once a vital consideration in the planning of school buildings, with books written as far back as the late 19th century focusing on the importance of daylight in the classroom.

E Many in this part of the country freely admit how difficult it is to get ready for the day ahead, several hours before the sun comes up.

F However, despite the apparent simplicity of the theory, little research has been done on the effects of light in schools, so not all of them are keen to change their lighting systems.

G Therefore, it seemed on the face of it that there was nothing to lose.

Part 7

You are going to read five reviews of songs by teenage boy bands. For questions **43–52,** choose from the reviews (**A–E**). The reviews may be chosen more than once.

Mark your answers **on the separate answer sheet**.

Which review

mentions that the song was the best the band released?	**43**	
says the song's lyrics are surprisingly effective when performed?	**44**	
says some instruments cannot be clearly heard?	**45**	
says the song has wide appeal despite its style?	**46**	
suggests the track deserved to have been appreciated more?	**47**	
says that the track has not lost any of its originality?	**48**	
mentions an opportunity for everyone in the band to display their singing ability?	**49**	
mentions the influence someone outside the band had on its music?	**50**	
says that the song is easy to relate to?	**51**	
admires a voice that is not what it seems?	**52**	

Reviews of songs by teenage boy bands

A *Fran*, by The Warts

A significant problem faced by boy bands is the narrow musical range expected of them. On the one hand, there's pop-rock, on the other, a dull version of rhythm and blues. Anything that differs from those styles sounds wildly creative, which may explain the phenomenal success of The Wart's hit song *Fran* in the music charts. The keyboard plays a central role on this track, giving it a sad feel. The lyrics are cleverly written, with each song-line starting with the last word of the previous line. This is more impressive than you might think just reading about it, because each band member takes a line in turn. It's a showcase for The Warts' excellent voices, and lead singer Mike Royce is outstanding.

B *Hard Shell*, by Loud

Loud specialised in disco music until three years ago, when a new producer was brought in who gave them a completely different sound. This has resulted in a string of recent hits although their latest song, *Hard Shell*, is heavy with electronic synthesizers, string instruments and horns. Ned Laing leads on vocals, guitarist Grant Berry manages a creditable solo, and the band's rhythm section is faultless. But at just two-and-a-half minutes long, it's over before you know it. And sadly, the song lacks the memorable lyrics of their earlier successes. In the end, it seems to have proved too polished for their younger fans, and too lightweight for the older ones. It hasn't been a hit, though many in the industry feel it should have been.

C *What I Lost*, by Dealt

Though Dealt got together to compete with other popular boy bands, their first single, *What I Lost*, had few of the elements that defined boy band music at the time: none of the sophisticated disco beats that might have been expected. Instead, it's understated rhythm and blues with a trace of folk, and accented by that least cool of instruments, the accordion. It was a fantastic debut; four years later, it's still unique, as different from the usual boy-band style as accordions are from electronic synthesisers, though both were used on the song. And although the subject matter, romance, is familiar, there's a clever twist: *What I Lost* is set in a courtroom. It was a track that was hard to improve on, and they never did.

D *No Grace*, by the Bowls

Boy band The Bowls' hit song *No Grace* features Len Blane's gentle lead vocals and flowing harmonies from some of the other band members. Say what you like about Blane, but there's no doubt that he has a gift for writing poetic love songs and arranging them to music. *No Grace*, which he claims to have written in an afternoon, is one of his finest songs. It's become a classic guilty pleasure for many people who wouldn't normally admit to liking a soft-pop love song – but why feel guilty? There's something touching about the lyrics and they deal with themes that everyone will have experienced at some time in their lives.

E *Floss*, by Slog

Released while Slog were at their short-lived peak, their hit song *Floss* is a splendid example of attitude plus technology. It opens with a drum solo, which gives way to three minutes of keyboard craziness that sounds like something a far more experimental band might have come up with. The three Slog members play conventional guitars and drums, but it's virtually impossible to detect them over the unusual electronic sounds of the backing track. Then there's lead singer Mo Aramba's remarkable vocals – more those of a thirty-year-old, than of a boy of seventeen. *Floss* is a marvellous track, and an inspiration for boy bands everywhere.

WRITING (1 hour 20 minutes)

Part 1

You **must** answer this question. Write your answer in **140–190** words in an appropriate style **on the separate answer sheet**.

---

1 In your English class you have been talking about decisions which teenagers sometimes have to make. Now your English teacher has asked you to write an essay for homework.

Write your essay using **all** the notes and giving reasons for your point of view.

Is it better for teenagers to make their own decisions or to ask for advice from other people?

Notes

Write about:

1. deciding which subjects to study
2. choosing clothes
3. .... (your own idea)

Part 2

Write an answer to **one** of the questions **2–4** in this part. Write your answer in **140–190** words in an appropriate style **on the separate answer sheet**. Put the question number in the box at the top of the answer sheet.

---

2 You see this announcement in an international e-magazine about the environment:

> *Articles wanted*
>
> **Inventions and the environment**
>
> In your opinion, which invention has had a good effect on the environment and which invention has had a bad effect? Why?
>
> The best articles will appear online next week.

Write your **article**.

3 You have received this email from your English friend, Naomi:

> Hi – my family's moving house next month. I know you moved house recently, too, so do you have any advice for me? I'm also a bit worried about living in a new area and making new friends.
> Have you got any suggestions?
>
> Thanks
>
> Naomi

Write your **email**.

4 You have seen this announcement in a new English-language magazine for schools:

> **Stories wanted**
>
> We are looking for stories for our new English-language magazine for teenagers. Your story must **begin** with this sentence:
>
> *Jess opened the envelope, wondering who it could be from.*
>
> Your story must include:
> - an invitation
> - a surprise

Write your **story**.

LISTENING (approximately 40 minutes)

Part 1

You will hear people talking in eight different situations.

For questions **1–8**, choose the best answer (**A**, **B** or **C**).

---

1 You hear a singer talking about performing on stage.

What does she do if she feels nervous before a performance?

A She pretends the audience is not there.

B She talks with other people in her group.

C She uses a technique suggested by a colleague.

2 You hear a girl telling her father about a special day at school.

How did she feel?

A surprised to be asked for her views

B excited about meeting someone well known

C pleased that her talents were recognised

3 You hear two friends talking about a summer camp they could both go on.

What would they both find difficult about going on it?

A being away from home

B getting on with other people

C doing the organised activities

4 You hear a boy talking about his favourite TV programme.

How does he feel about it?

A disappointed by the absence of one important element

B surprised by the references to real historical figures

C confused by the way the characters behave

5 You hear a journalist talking about an unusual type of house.

What does he think of it?

A He's impressed by how original the design is.

B He's confident that it could be successful elsewhere.

C He's keen to experience staying in it himself.

6 You hear part of an interview with a boy called Max, who found a prehistoric object.

What effect has the discovery had on Max's life?

A It's made him more confident.

B It's provided him with a new interest.

C It's changed the way his friends treat him.

7 You hear a girl talking about the sport called netball.

What does she say about it?

A The rules are quite complicated.

B The skills are difficult to acquire.

C The level of fitness needed is surprising.

8 You hear two friends discussing a news story about some rock climbers.

How does the boy feel about it?

A He feels sorry for the families of the climbers.

B He admires the courage the climbers showed.

C He's determined to follow the climbers' example.

Part 2

You will hear a woman called Ingrid talking about doing volunteer work on a shark conservation project on the island of Fiji. For questions **9–18**, complete the sentences with a word or short phrase.

Shark conservation project on Fiji

Ingrid first came across information about the shark project in a **(9)** .... report.

Ingrid was taught how to dive in a **(10)** .... near her home.

Ingrid says she'll never forget the **(11)** .... on the day she arrived in Fiji.

Ingrid uses the word **(12)** .... to describe her experience of seeing sharks while diving.

Ingrid says that the **(13)** .... of the Bull Sharks was what impressed her most.

Ingrid was pleased to be able to dive to a depth of **(14)** .... metres.

Ingrid mainly worked with researchers who were collecting information about the shark **(15)** .... in the local area.

Ingrid helped researchers to attach metal tags to **(16)** .... Bull Sharks in order to track where they go.

Ingrid was disappointed that she never saw a **(17)** .... Shark.

Ingrid has kept in touch with someone from **(18)** .... , who she met on the project.

Part 3

You will hear five short extracts in which teenagers are talking about their experience of doing experiments in science lessons at school. For questions **19–23**, choose from the list (**A–H**) how each speaker feels about their experience. Use the letters only once. There are three extra letters which you do not need to use.

A bored by having to do things many times

B proud of their ability to be adaptable

C frustrated that important work had to be done too quickly

D inspired by the feedback that was given

E embarrassed by the mistakes that were made

F relieved that the results were better than expected

G disappointed by the lack of support from the teacher

H irritated by someone's lack of organisation

Speaker 1		**19**
Speaker 2		**20**
Speaker 3		**21**
Speaker 4		**22**
Speaker 5		**23**

Part 4

You will hear an interview with an air traffic controller called Jake Watson, whose job involves directing aircraft in and out of an airport. For questions **24–30**, choose the best answer (**A**, **B** or **C**).

---

24 What does Jake find most challenging about his job?

A communicating with a variety of people

B focusing on several tasks at the same time

C being responsible for aircraft safety

25 Why did Jake decide to become an air traffic controller?

A He hoped to increase his income.

B He felt the need to do something different.

C He was unable to fulfil his dream of becoming a commercial pilot.

26 Jake says the selection process for the job showed him that

A he was stronger in some skills than he'd thought.

B he'd be able to develop skills he already had.

C he needed to learn a number of new skills.

27 Jake says the first time he worked without supervision, he

A wished he was still being monitored.

B felt completely ready to deal with it.

C was too busy to let it worry him at all.

28 Jake says that when no planes are flying due to fog, controllers

A use equipment to assess possible solutions to the problem.

B work harder than usual to monitor changing conditions.

C take advantage of a break from their normal routine.

29 What does Jake say about flight delays?

A He finds them irritating when he's a passenger himself.

B He avoids thinking about passengers' problems when he's working.

C He thinks passengers should be given clearer information.

30 How did Jake feel during a recent air display?

A relieved that plans for the day were successful

B concerned about the number of people watching

C impressed by the impact it had on the airport

SPEAKING (14 minutes)

You take the Speaking test with another candidate (possibly two candidates), referred to here as your partner. There are two examiners. One will speak to you and your partner and the other will be listening. Both examiners will award marks.

Part 1 (2 minutes (3 minutes for groups of three))

The examiner asks you and your partner questions about yourselves. You may be asked about things like 'your home town', 'your interests', 'your career plans', etc.

Part 2 (4 minutes (6 minutes for groups of three))

The examiner gives you two photographs and asks you to talk about them for one minute. The examiner then asks your partner a question about your photographs and your partner responds briefly.

Then the examiner gives your partner two different photographs. Your partner talks about these photographs for one minute. This time the examiner asks you a question about your partner's photographs and you respond briefly.

Part 3 (4 minutes (5 minutes for groups of three))

The examiner asks you and your partner to talk together. They give you a task to look at so you can think about and discuss an idea, giving reasons for your opinion. For example, you may be asked to think about some changes in the world, or about spending free time with your family. After you have discussed the task for about two minutes with your partner, the examiner will ask you a follow-up question, which you should discuss for a further minute.

Part 4 (4 minutes (6 minutes for groups of three))

The examiner asks some further questions, which leads to a more general discussion of what you have talked about in Part 3. You may comment on your partner's answers if you wish.

Test 2

READING AND USE OF ENGLISH (1 hour 15 minutes)

Part 1

For questions **1–8**, read the text below and decide which answer (**A**, **B**, **C** or **D**) best fits each gap. There is an example at the beginning (**0**).

Mark your answers **on the separate answer sheet.**

Example:

0 **A** gone along **B** come up **C** thought out **D** looked into

0	A	B	C	D
	▭	▬	▭	▭

Magic paper?

Scientists have **(0)** .... with a new type of paper that can be printed on and then used again up to 20 times. Users will be able to either remove the writing from the paper themselves, or **(1)** .... it to disappear over a period of time, after which the paper will be completely blank and ready to be printed on again. There is no significant change in quality between the first and the twentieth printout. Under normal **(2)** .... it seems that the writing will remain perfectly **(3)** .... for at least three days, long enough for most **(4)** .... purposes.

This new process does not **(5)** .... ink. Instead, the paper is printed on using a combination of chemicals and light. If users want the print to disappear more quickly, they can apply heat to the paper. This can take as little as ten minutes. The **(6)** .... is that in the future this paper will be **(7)** .... used, providing an environmentally friendly **(8)** .... to ordinary paper.

1	**A**	make	**B**	cause	**C**	expect	**D**	leave
2	**A**	situations	**B**	circumstances	**C**	contexts	**D**	settings
3	**A**	clear	**B**	obvious	**C**	evident	**D**	apparent
4	**A**	objective	**B**	practical	**C**	functional	**D**	constructive
5	**A**	insist	**B**	request	**C**	oblige	**D**	require
6	**A**	cause	**B**	wish	**C**	hope	**D**	reason
7	**A**	widely	**B**	broadly	**C**	largely	**D**	mainly
8	**A**	substitute	**B**	option	**C**	replacement	**D**	alternative

Part 2

For questions **9–16**, read the text below and think of the word which best fits each gap. Use only **one** word in each gap. There is an example at the beginning **(0)**.

Write your answers **IN CAPITAL LETTERS on the separate answer sheet**.

Example: | 0 | O N E |

The Freedom Ship

Imagine the largest ship you've ever seen, then try to imagine **(0)** .... far bigger. In fact, try to imagine a ship **(9)** .... size of a small island and big **(10)** .... to provide a permanent home for around 40,000 residents. Imagine this ship circling the globe once every two years, spending 70% of the time close to major cities and the rest following the warm weather as **(11)** .... sails between countries.

This was the aim of the designers of the Freedom Ship, **(12)** .... dream it was to create a vast floating city, complete **(13)** .... hospitals, schools, shops and even an airport. First proposed in 1994, it has been advertised as a new way of living, a unique lifestyle in a global community **(14)** .... suit all budgets. However, such an elaborate plan comes at an extremely high price. **(15)** .... a result, the designers have been unable to **(16)** .... their exciting ideas into practice. But who can tell what possibilities the future holds?

Part 3

For questions **17–24**, read the text below. Use the word given in capitals at the end of some of the lines to form a word that fits in the gap **in the same line**. There is an example at the beginning (**0**).

Write your answers **IN CAPITAL LETTERS on the separate answer sheet.**

Example: | 0 | A W A R E N E S S |

New Yorkers jump on giant bed

In New York, a man decided to make a video to raise **(0)** .... for	**AWARE**
a children's charity. His **(17)** .... was also to spread joy in a city	**INTEND**
which sometimes has a reputation for being cold and **(18)** .... So	**WELCOME**
he transported a giant bed around town and encouraged his fellow	
(19) .... to jump on it, then watched with	**CITY**
(20) .... as large numbers of people did so. Those who were more	**SATISFY**
(21) .... started to see which of their friends could jump the highest	**COMPETE**
in preference to just jumping up and down.	
His first thought had been just to use a mattress, but then a friend built a	
proper frame with the **(22)** .... to support six adults jumping around	**STRONG**
at the same time. He was afraid of getting a negative **(23)** .... from	**RESPOND**
some people who would think the idea was silly and **(24)** .... and	**CHILD**
refuse to do it. Most people who tried it, however, said the experience	
was really enjoyable and that they'd happily do it again!	

Part 4

For questions **25–30**, complete the second sentence so that it has a similar meaning to the first sentence, using the word given. **Do not change the word given**. You must use between **two** and **five** words, including the word given. Here is an example (**0**).

Example:

0 Prizes are given out when the school year finishes.

PLACE

Prize-giving .... end of the school year.

The gap can be filled by the words 'takes place at the', so you write:

Example:	**0**	*TAKES PLACE AT THE*

Write **only** the missing words **IN CAPITAL LETTERS on the separate answer sheet.**

---

25 I think I can come to your party after all.

SHOULD

I .... to your party after all.

26 Last year, the number of complaints about the leisure centre rose.

INCREASE

Last year, there .... the number of complaints about the leisure centre.

27 Marta always starts to talk about something else when I try to discuss the history project with her.

SUBJECT

Marta changes .... time I try to discuss the history project with her.

28 There will be bikes available for you to use during the school trip.

DISPOSAL

There will be bikes .... during the school trip.

29 My geography teacher expects a lot from us, so I'm working hard on this project.

EXPECTATIONS

My geography teacher .... of us, so I'm working hard on this project.

30 Sorry, I completely forgot the time so I missed the bus.

REALISE

Sorry, I .... the time was so I missed the bus.

Part 5

You are going to read an article about an astronomy club in the USA. For questions **31–36**, choose the answer (**A**, **B**, **C** or **D**) which you think fits best according to the text.

Mark your answers **on the separate answer sheet.**

A special astronomy club

A group of US teenagers study the night sky.

The teenage members of the Earth to Sky Calculus Club live in and around Bishop, a mountain town in the USA surrounded almost entirely by wilderness, to the east of the Sierra Nevada mountain range. Over the last few years, this isolated group has launched over 50 balloons to the edge of space, around 35 km above the Earth's surface. It's a long-running science project but with a bit of a twist: it's part astronomy experiment, part backcountry adventure, which is possibly why teenagers get involved. I join them one weekend in late spring. They are about to release a high-altitude balloon, hoping to record shooting stars. These occur when a rock or piece of metal travelling through space enters the Earth's atmosphere, producing a trail of light.

As it gets dark, the teenagers secure a soft insulated $5 lunch box to the bottom of the balloon. Inside is a camera, an instrument to measure altitude and a thermometer to gauge the changes along the ascent. Two GPS trackers are mounted on the outside of the lunch box to help the group to find it later. A gas tank, donated by an enthusiast in a neighbouring state, is used to inflate the balloon, which slowly grows to the size of a small car. An older boy had made a seven-hour round trip to get hold of it. 'I didn't really mind,' he says. Anyway, for kids in this club, that's a given.

Finally, it's time for lift-off. 'Five, four, three, two, one,' they chant, and the balloon begins its ascent. Some of them run and track its path with powerful flashlights for as long as they are able, illuminating the creamy orb in the moonless sky. There is quiet, and a palpable sense of collective wonder. Then the balloon disappears into the night.

When the launch is over, most of the students go home, but a few stay to watch the shooting stars. A boy climbs into a sleeping bag and promptly falls asleep. 'We're the only ones talking,' says one girl in hushed tones. 'I know,' whispers another. A meteor shoots across the middle of the sky.

As a balloon rises, the air pressure lessens and the balloon expands until it's almost the size of a house. Then it pops in a dramatic explosion. A parachute helps the equipment inside the lunch box land safely back on Earth. The students will find it the following day, using the GPS trackers as a guide. Getting it back isn't straightforward, but that's part of the appeal. There is little inhabited land around Bishop, so the lunch box almost always lands somewhere in the middle of nowhere. 'To me, recoveries are a huge part of the program,' said the group's leader, who notes they've lost only two lunch boxes in 53 launches. 'Part of the journey has been becoming more familiar with this landscape in a way you never normally would.'

On this occasion, the lunch box had landed 84 km west of Bishop, but to get to it, the recovery team would have to drive south of the Sierra and then back up the western side of the mountain range. Then they'd have to agree whether driving or walking would be preferable – things could turn treacherous if the lunch box was on a high peak, or even worse, up a very tall tree. 'It's important to keep in mind that these students are native to the Eastern Sierra,' their leader says. 'What may seem wild and perilous to some, is simply a way of life to others.'

In the end, it took them 11 hours to find the lunch box. It was in a canyon, high on a flat rock, in the middle of a cascading waterfall. The camera hadn't recorded any shooting stars. Sure, it's a bit of a disappointment, but it's one more tale of adventure to share with anyone who asks.

31 What does the writer say about the club in the first paragraph?

A The combination of activities offered makes it unusual.
B Its members have joined because there's little else to do.
C The projects it organises are over-ambitious.
D Its aims remain rather unclear.

32 What does 'it' refer to in line 29?

A the lunch box
B the balloon
C the gas tank
D the car

33 How does the writer say the group feel when the balloon takes off?

A disappointed to lose sight of it
B amazed that it has risen so quickly
C hopeful that they will recover it
D moved by the experience of it

34 What view does the group's leader express in the fifth paragraph?

A The recovery operations can be inconvenient.
B Learning so much about the area has been a bonus.
C The long journeys they make are annoying but necessary.
D Losing some lunch boxes has been a price worth paying.

35 What does 'things could turn treacherous' mean in line 68?

A The teenagers could appear irresponsible.
B The situation could put people at risk.
C The outcome could be unpredictable.
D Their efforts could prove inadequate.

36 What point is made in the sixth paragraph?

A People should respect the lifestyles of the inhabitants of an area.
B People have to make difficult decisions at some stage in their lives.
C People adopt attitudes that are affected by the environment they grow up in.
D People should exercise more caution when in unfamiliar environments.

Part 6

You are going to read an article about some seals that are using technology to their advantage. Six sentences have been removed from the article. Choose from the sentences **A–G** the one which fits each gap (**37–42**). There is one extra sentence which you do not need to use.

Mark your answers **on the separate answer sheet.**

Clever seals

Scientists believe some seals have discovered a new way to hunt for fish.

Tiny electronic devices attached to wild animals have become an increasingly common way for scientists to study those that are difficult to locate and follow on a day-to-day basis. The devices, known as 'acoustic tags', send out signals in the form of sound waves that the human ear cannot hear. The animals to which they are attached cannot hear them either, so are not disturbed by them. However, now it seems that clever seals are using them to their advantage to catch fish!

This finding was revealed in a recent study published by a team of researchers from the University of St. Andrews in Scotland. **37** ______ Previous research by another team had also indicated that while the sounds produced by acoustic tags could not be heard by the fish they were attached to, other animals that hunted the fish, like seals and sea lions, were able to detect the signal quite easily.

To verify if that was true, the St. Andrews University researchers selected a group of ten young grey seals that had been born in captivity and never lived in the wild. This meant that the marine animals had never encountered the ocean. **38** ______ The researchers placed the seals one at a time inside a pool that contained 20 boxes, only two of which contained fish – one with tags and the other without.

Each seal was allowed to enter the pool on a number of occasions to explore the boxes. In order to ensure that the seals were not depending on their memory, the fish were randomly moved to different boxes each time. There was initially no difference in the amount of time it took the seals to discover the tagged and untagged fish. **39** ______

What was even more interesting was that the more 'experienced' the seals became, the more frequently they visited the box containing the tagged fish. **40** ______

To confirm that the animals were in fact making use of the tags, the researchers conducted a second experiment using two boxes – one containing pieces of fish and the other just acoustic tags. **41** ______

While this experiment involved only seals, the researchers believe that other marine mammals may also be using the information to avoid predators. They are worried that sharks, for example, which have been tagged by scientists may be negatively affected, as the signals emitted by the acoustic tags could warn smaller animals of their presence and so prevent the sharks from catching their prey. Apart from messing up nature's food chain, another potential concern relating to the use of acoustic tags has arisen. **42** ______ Now that the secret is out, scientists will have to come up with another innovative way to conduct their studies – one that cannot be detected by clever marine animals.

A Nor had they been exposed to any kind of acoustic tag.

B It is that the conclusions reached by previous fish studies may not be reliable.

C This suggested that the seals had indeed figured out how to use the acoustic signals to their advantage.

D Nevertheless, this behaviour led the team to doubt whether their theory was correct.

E They had become interested in the idea that the tags might be having unexpected effects.

F Sure enough, the seals all went to the one that was sending out signals.

G However, after they had been in the pool a few times, they started locating the tagged fish much faster.

Part 7

You are going to read an article in which young people talk about their early experiences of going to football matches. For questions **43–52**, choose from the people (**A–D**). The people may be chosen more than once.

Mark your answers **on the separate answer sheet**.

Which person

says that one player was initially unsure of his success?	**43**	
says that they missed a big event in their team's history?	**44**	
was given a special treat to mark an amazing achievement?	**45**	
felt being a spectator gave them a sense of belonging?	**46**	
expresses admiration for a footballer on the other side?	**47**	
says they went to football matches on a regular basis?	**48**	
mentions that a member of their team showed great confidence regarding a match result?	**49**	
enjoyed an event they saw during the match more than the final outcome?	**50**	
has a lasting memory of viewing the pitch from high up?	**51**	
witnessed one of the early matches played by a very promising team member?	**52**	

Football matches

A Phoebe

It would have been impossible for a 10-year-old taken to the football stadium every other weekend, as I was, not to get sucked in by the atmosphere in the stands and out on the pitch. And to stand among the crowd of spectators was like being welcomed into one great big family. There was a heightened sense of glamour, too, as we had a player in our team who'd also played internationally. To me, he seemed to have been sent from another universe. Anyway, at least I got to witness some of the club's glory years, even though my first match was a whole two seasons after they'd won a major cup. Still, plenty of great memories – luckily, because the club hasn't done so well in recent years.

B Mark

I've been going to football matches ever since I was about six. When I think back, I can't remember the player's names so well, but I do remember that our best goal scorer, when I first started going, was a tall agile guy who'd just curl the ball into the back of the net. On one occasion he slammed it into the goal from 40 metres away before the goalkeeper even had time to raise his hands. I've never seen a better goal since, although I only got a really good view of it because my dad led us up the wrong steps in the stand, after the half-time break. It was followed by the best celebration: a fantastic pointing-at-the-skies moment. We won 2-1 but, to be honest, after that amazing spectacle, nothing else really mattered. Dad bought me a celebratory burger on the way home.

C Thomas

The first time I went to a football match was quite an experience. The club I supported had just knocked out the favourites from a national tournament, and every time I turned on the radio I heard our captain telling the press that the cup was as good as ours. There were 40,000 people packed into the stadium, but it was seeing the floodlit grounds below from the top of the steeply arranged seats that stuck in my mind. That was the moment I really fell in love with football. And then they kicked off. My team lost – a word combination I quickly got used to. That time it was due to one brilliant player scoring from 25 metres. Then his second goal went in and the final score was 2-1 to them. It was still amazing as far as I was concerned.

D Teresa

On my first ever visit to the stadium, my team were playing on a muddy pitch that got worse as the rain kept falling. But that didn't put one player off – a teenager who'd recently come up from the youth team and later went on to achieve great fame. He scored our only goal in the final minutes. I vaguely recall the ball bouncing over the goalkeeper, who'd come out to the edge of his area. He ran back and dived for it but slipped in the mud and couldn't keep it out of the net. The weather was so bad, the teenager could barely see what had happened and didn't realise at first that he'd actually scored. So there we go – pouring rain, muddy pitch, 5-1 defeat for my team, got soaked. And I still decided to support them!

WRITING (1 hour 20 minutes)

Part 1

You **must** answer this question. Write your answer in **140–190** words in an appropriate style **on the separate answer sheet**.

---

1 In your English class you have been talking about rules at home. Now your English teacher has asked you to write an essay for homework.

Write your essay using **all** the notes and giving reasons for your point of view.

'It's very important for young people to have rules at home.'

Do you agree?

Notes

Write about:

1. jobs around the house
2. behaviour during meal-times
3. .... (your own idea)

Part 2

Write an answer to **one** of the questions **2–4** in this part. Write your answer in **140–190** words in an appropriate style **on the separate answer sheet**. Put the question number in the box at the top of the answer sheet.

---

2 You have received this email from your English friend, Sam:

> Hi
>
> A friend of mine never seems to want to do the same things as I do, and I always end up doing things I'm not that interested in. I'm not sure what I should do about this as we actually get on really well with each other.
>
> Can you give me some advice?
>
> Thanks
>
> Sam

Write your **email**.

3 You recently saw this notice in an international magazine for teenagers:

> *Reviews wanted*
>
> **Family holidays**
>
> Do you know a good place to have a family holiday? If so, write us a review describing the place, explaining the benefits for different members of a family and saying why you especially recommend it.
>
> The best reviews will be published next month.

Write your **review**.

4 You have seen this announcement in an international magazine for schools:

> **Stories wanted**
>
> We are looking for stories for our new English-language magazine for teenagers. Your story must **begin** with this sentence:
>
> *Mark was walking along the beach one Saturday morning.*
>
> Your story must include:
> - a sound
> - a rescue

Write your **story**.

LISTENING (approximately 40 minutes)

Part 1

You will hear people talking in eight different situations.

For questions **1–8**, choose the best answer (**A**, **B** or **C**).

---

1 You hear two friends talking about a lesson on the subject of newspapers.

What do they agree about it?

A Some unusual ideas were expressed.

B A wide range of issues were covered.

C It was well-planned.

2 You hear a man talking about skateboarders in the past.

What is he doing?

A explaining the reputation they once had

B describing how attitudes towards them have changed

C suggesting reasons for their interest in the sport

3 You hear a girl talking about a diary she keeps.

Her main aim is to explain

A her reason for starting to write a diary.

B the effect that keeping a diary has on her.

C the different functions a diary can have.

4 You hear a boy talking about a weekly video he posts online in which he expresses his opinions.

What does he find most challenging?

A responding to criticism from other people

B producing original ideas on a regular basis

C coping with the amount of interest he gets

5 You hear part of a programme about sea creatures called sea dragons.

What does the man say about the different types of sea dragon?

A Their sources of food are becoming scarcer.

B They have names which reflect their appearance.

C Certain differences between them have only recently been discovered.

6 You hear two friends talking about a film they've seen.

What does the girl think about it?

A The storyline was too complicated to follow.

B The music was unsuitable for the subject matter.

C The main actor failed to live up to her expectations.

7 You hear a news item about a small town in Alaska called Whittier.

What is unusual about the town?

A Children can get to school without going outdoors.

B There is only one shop for the people to use.

C All residents live and work in one tall apartment block.

8 You hear two friends talking about a dance competition.

What do they agree about it?

A It should be held on another day.

B It will be more fun to watch than take part in.

C It's bound to be a great success.

Part 2

You will hear an astronomer called Steve Mitchell talking about his work. For questions **9–18**, complete the sentences with a word or short phrase.

Working as an astronomer

Steve first became interested in astronomy after watching a **(9)** .... on TV.

Steve says that as a teenager he particularly appreciated the **(10)** .... of the night sky.

Steve describes how excited he felt when he saw a **(11)** .... through his telescope.

Steve finds it surprising that the **(12)** .... in the universe are so varied.

Steve's ambition is to go on a trip to **(13)** .... one day.

Steve says that **(14)** .... can cause unexpected problems for inexperienced astronomers living in built-up areas.

Steve thinks finding a **(15)** .... is the best thing that beginners interested in astronomy could do.

Steve thinks the many **(16)** .... surrounding one planet would be easy for young astronomers to identify.

Steve says that amateur astronomers' important **(17)** .... include finding new stars.

Steve explains that **(18)** .... is the most important quality astronomers need to have.

Part 3

You will hear five short extracts in which teenagers are talking about a favourite book. For questions **19–23**, choose from the list **(A–H)** what each speaker says about the book. Use the letters only once. There are three extra letters which you do not need to use.

A I was drawn into it from the beginning.

B It's more humorous than other books by the same author.

C One of the characters reminds me of someone I know well.

D It used to belong to a relative of mine.

E It's set in a place I've visited.

F I was inspired to read it by a TV programme.

G It helped me to deal with a situation in my own life.

H There are interesting descriptions of people in it.

Speaker 1		**19**
Speaker 2		**20**
Speaker 3		**21**
Speaker 4		**22**
Speaker 5		**23**

Part 4

You will hear an interview with a man called Josh Reed, who teaches people how to climb trees. For questions **24–30**, choose the best answer (**A**, **B** or **C**).

---

24 When Josh tells people what he does, they are usually

A confused about what his job involves.

B surprised that there is such a job.

C critical of his choice of job.

25 What appealed to Josh as a child about climbing trees?

A the excitement of doing something his parents disapproved of

B the chance to face up to a physical challenge

C the contrast with his other daily activities

26 What does Josh think now about the job he had looking after trees in public places?

A He continued doing it for too long.

B It was the obvious work for him to go into.

C The training he received for it was limited.

27 Josh says his main aim in offering his tree-climbing courses was to

A make people more knowledgeable about trees.

B show people the health benefits of this activity.

C change people's attitude to the environment.

28 Why is Josh against climbing very tall trees?

A It's dangerous for ordinary people to try it.

B It's unfair to disturb the wildlife in them.

C It's wrong to run the risk of damaging them.

29 What impressed Josh about the group he recently taught?

A how effectively they dealt with a problem

B how carefully they listened to his advice

C how quickly they learnt climbing skills

30 What does Josh look forward to doing in the future?

A developing new tree-climbing techniques

B having the chance to climb trees in different parts of the world

C spending more time promoting tree climbing as a leisure activity

SPEAKING (14 minutes)

You take the Speaking test with another candidate (possibly two candidates), referred to here as your partner. There are two examiners. One will speak to you and your partner and the other will be listening. Both examiners will award marks.

Part 1 (2 minutes (3 minutes for groups of three))

The examiner asks you and your partner questions about yourselves. You may be asked about things like 'your home town', 'your interests', 'your career plans', etc.

Part 2 (4 minutes (6 minutes for groups of three))

The examiner gives you two photographs and asks you to talk about them for one minute. The examiner then asks your partner a question about your photographs and your partner responds briefly.

Then the examiner gives your partner two different photographs. Your partner talks about these photographs for one minute. This time the examiner asks you a question about your partner's photographs and you respond briefly.

Part 3 (4 minutes (5 minutes for groups of three))

The examiner asks you and your partner to talk together. They give you a task to look at so you can think about and discuss an idea, giving reasons for your opinion. For example, you may be asked to think about some changes in the world, or about spending free time with your family. After you have discussed the task for about two minutes with your partner, the examiner will ask you a follow-up question, which you should discuss for a further minute.

Part 4 (4 minutes (6 minutes for groups of three))

The examiner asks some further questions, which leads to a more general discussion of what you have talked about in Part 3. You may comment on your partner's answers if you wish.

Test 3

READING AND USE OF ENGLISH (1 hour 15 minutes)

Part 1

For questions **1–8**, read the text below and decide which answer (**A**, **B**, **C** or **D**) best fits each gap. There is an example at the beginning (**0**).

Mark your answers **on the separate answer sheet.**

Example:

0 **A** far **B** alike **C** even **D** again

0	A	B	C	D
	▭	▭	▬	▭

Clever crows

Did you know that crows are really intelligent birds, maybe **(0)** .... as intelligent as young children? Scientists have **(1)** .... at this conclusion following a series of experiments **(2)** .... in the UK and New Zealand. In one, a crow worked out how to use tools to **(3)** .... an eight-stage puzzle and find food that had been placed out of **(4)** .... The crow had never seen the complex puzzle before but managed to solve it in a **(5)** .... short time, which is something many young children would **(6)** .... to do. In another experiment, six crows had to carry **(7)** .... various tasks. In one task, the birds had to learn that if they dropped heavy objects into tubes filled with water, the water level would rise, **(8)** .... them to catch food rewards floating on the surface. The crows soon understood that the most effective way of doing this was to choose tubes with high water levels and to select objects that would sink.

1	**A** approached	**B** come	**C** got	**D** arrived
2	**A** adopted	**B** conducted	**C** operated	**D** established
3	**A** conclude	**B** decide	**C** complete	**D** secure
4	**A** reach	**B** access	**C** way	**D** limit
5	**A** commonly	**B** relatively	**C** generally	**D** routinely
6	**A** compete	**B** fight	**C** struggle	**D** challenge
7	**A** on	**B** through	**C** off	**D** out
8	**A** enabling	**B** letting	**C** ensuring	**D** confirming

Part 2

For questions **9–16**, read the text below and think of the word which best fits each gap. Use only **one** word in each gap. There is an example at the beginning (**0**).

Write your answers **IN CAPITAL LETTERS on the separate answer sheet.**

Example: | **0** | T O |

Young snowboarder

Meet Jack Preston, the latest – and youngest – star on the snowboarding scene. He's won competitions, regularly competes against adults and hopes **(0)** .... compete in the next Winter Olympics, but he's only 12 years old. According to his trainer, there are professional snowboarders who may never achieve **(9)** .... he has, and it is no exaggeration to say he's the best young snowboarder in the country. Jack's inspired by his parents, keen snowboarders themselves, **(10)** .... first introduced him to snowboarding **(11)** .... a very young age. Jack took to the sport naturally and was soon racing down the slopes. **(12)** .... then, his snowboarding has gone from strength to strength and he now **(13)** .... much of his free time practising and travelling around the world to **(14)** .... part in competitions. His parents make sure this doesn't interfere **(15)** .... his school life and Jack says he's grateful for the opportunity to **(16)** .... so many great experiences. Keep an eye out for Jack Preston at the next Winter Olympics!

Part 3

For questions **17–24**, read the text below. Use the word given in capitals at the end of some of the lines to form a word that fits in the gap **in the same line**. There is an example at the beginning (**0**).

Write your answers **IN CAPITAL LETTERS on the separate answer sheet.**

Example: | 0 | N A T U R A L |

Oregon's Lost Lake

In Oregon in the US there's a **(0)** ……… wonder called Lost Lake.	**NATURE**
During winter, it looks like any other large lake. However, in late	
spring the water **(17)** ……… , transforming the 'lake' into a beautiful	**APPEAR**
field of grass. This may seem **(18)** ……… , but in fact there's a logical	**MYSTERY**
(19) ……… : the lake lies on an ancient volcano, and there is a	**EXPLAIN**
continuous flow of water through a tunnel in the lake bed created	
by lava, the hot, liquid rock that came out of the volcano when it	
was **(20)** ……… .	**ACT**
The lake fills up **(21)** ……… during the rainy season in autumn.	**STEADY**
Because the lava tunnel measures less than two metres in diameter, the	
water is **(22)** ……… to escape quickly, so there's more water coming	**ABLE**
into the lake than leaving it. That's why the lake fills up, reaching a	
maximum **(23)** ……… of fifty metres. It remains full as snow from	**DEEP**
the **(24)** ……… mountains melts. But once the snow has disappeared,	**SURROUND**
the gradual loss of water causes the lake to vanish.	

Part 4

For questions **25–30**, complete the second sentence so that it has a similar meaning to the first sentence, using the word given. **Do not change the word given**. You must use between **two** and **five** words, including the word given. Here is an example (**0**).

Example:

0 Prizes are given out when the school year finishes.

PLACE

Prize-giving .... end of the school year.

The gap can be filled by the words 'takes place at the', so you write:

Example:	**0**	*TAKES PLACE AT THE*

Write only the missing words **IN CAPITAL LETTERS on the separate answer sheet.**

---

25 Don't ask Jim to join the football team – he really doesn't want to.

USE

It's .... Jim to join the football team – he really doesn't want to.

26 It's a pity I forgot to bring my coat with me, because it's absolutely freezing!

WISH

I .... to bring my coat with me, because it's absolutely freezing!

27 'You really shouldn't have upset your sister!' Dad said to me.

OFF

Dad told .... upsetting my sister.

28 Unfortunately, I don't know much about the history of the castles in the area.

UNFAMILIAR

Unfortunately, ... the history of the castles in this area.

29 They didn't expect many people would come to the beach party because of the weather.

EXPECTED

Few people .... up at the beach party because of the weather.

30 It's a pity Sarah didn't tell us which bus to take to her house.

OUGHT

Sarah .... us which bus to take to her house.

Part 5

You are going to read an extract from an interview with a palaeontologist, a scientist who studies dinosaurs and other creatures that lived millions of years ago. For questions **31–36**, choose the answer (**A**, **B**, **C** or **D**) which you think fits best according to the text.

Mark your answers **on the separate answer sheet.**

Walking with Dinosaurs

Chloe Morgan readily admits science, let alone Palaeontology, hadn't held too much appeal for her, at least not until she was fifteen. Even then, it happened more by accident than design. 'My younger brother was going through the dinosaur phase that's so common among children, and which I hadn't experienced. In fact, I tended to dismiss it. I reluctantly lent him a hand with a science project, and when I came across an article about some of the recent discoveries in the field, it just blew my mind. I knew immediately that this was something I wanted to commit myself to.'

I am curious to know what encouragement she got because Palaeontology was by no means a common career choice for young people at that time. 'I remember meeting my first professional palaeontologist,' she laughs. 'This guy, Matt Cornelius, was famous already, despite being quite young. At first I was a nervous wreck, even though he had a reputation for being approachable and easy-going. I was still worried he'd think I was just an annoying kid pestering him with my questions. But I felt more at ease when he showed so much patience and willingness to listen.'

I cannot resist bringing up the question of the portrayal of palaeontologists in movies and TV shows. Chloe frowns for a moment. 'I have to admit that films such as *Jurassic Park* featuring dinosaurs created by special effects technology have led to a huge surge in public interest in these creatures, though not necessarily in Palaeontology more generally. *line 37* However much I welcome this, I think the relatively few examples of palaeontologists depicted in the cinema are misleading. What irritates me is that we're either stereotyped as eccentric geniuses or rather geeky losers, figures of fun who don't know how to relate to people. And films fail to represent accurately the everyday reality of our working lives.' I ask her to explain.

'My job is remarkably varied. I spend lots of time digging up dinosaur bones, but I also have to put in long hours in laboratories, analysing fossils, and writing for scientific publications.'

While it's not necessarily something Chloe is required to do on a daily basis, there's also the question of communicating scientific findings to the public, if time allows. The role of explaining and clarifying is one she takes seriously. 'There are a lot of misunderstandings and misconceptions about science, and though I know colleagues who are reluctant to take on such a challenge and don't want to be distracted from doing research, I see dealing with these issues as something I ought to do. I like to reach out to young people in particular, because it's important to let them know about all aspects of science. Talking about dinosaurs is one way to get children fired up about the natural world, and widen their horizons. They *line 66* can start to appreciate other branches of science and to grasp more complex scientific ideas.'

The recent TV documentary *Walking with Dinosaurs* was a great opportunity for Chloe to influence the way dinosaurs are portrayed on screen, as she was invited to offer her advice. 'I had a fairly easy time of it because there was very little that I needed to comment on; it was mostly checking that the dinosaurs shown did exist together in the same time period. We succeeded in attracting audiences of all ages because we've learnt such a tremendous amount about dinosaurs recently.' This means that the dinosaurs in the documentary are easily the most life-like that have ever been portrayed.

Why does Chloe feel dinosaurs continue to fascinate us and remain the focus of ongoing research? 'I suspect that they speak to the innate explorer in all of us. Our imaginations are drawn to the unfamiliar and the prospect of discovery. And at a time when our world seems to be shrinking, prehistoric creatures remind us that there is still more out there to be discovered. And Palaeontology is a great form of time travel.'

31 Chloe says she became seriously interested in Palaeontology because

A she was astonished by something she read by chance.
B she had always been enthusiastic about related subjects.
C she was keen to share her brother's passion for the subject.
D she was aware that others seemed to know a great deal about it.

32 What does 'this' refer to in line 37?

A the number of films about dinosaurs
B the new desire for information about dinosaurs
C the greater public understanding of Palaeontology
D the special effects technology used by film makers

33 What does Chloe feel about the way palaeontologists are shown in films and on TV?

A disappointed that a false impression is given of them
B pleased because there is a range of different personalities
C resigned to putting up with the unfair criticism they receive
D amused by some of the situations they find themselves in

34 What does Chloe say about communicating with the public about Palaeontology?

A She is delighted she can devote so much time to it.
B She worries that it may prevent her from focusing on research.
C She is critical of some scientists' lack of ability to do it well.
D She feels it is her duty to make science more comprehensible.

35 What does the expression 'widen their horizons' mean in line 66?

A make them more tolerant of different things
B change their view of what's important in life
C make them aware of new ideas
D encourage them to travel more

36 Chloe thinks that dinosaurs continue to appeal to us because

A they make us appreciate that the world remains a mysterious place.
B they are creatures that it is hard to believe ever existed.
C they require interesting research in order for us to understand them.
D they provide an escape from the boredom of our everyday lives.

Part 6

You are going to read an article about the discovery of a new basic taste. Six sentences have been removed from the article. Choose from the sentences **A–G** the one which fits each gap (**37–42**). There is one extra sentence which you do not need to use.

Mark your answers **on the separate answer sheet.**

A new taste

Scientists believe they have found a new basic taste – beyond sour, sweet, salty, bitter and umami.

For hundreds of years, scientists have known about four basic, or 'primary' tastes: sour, sweet, salty and bitter. More recently, a Japanese chemist discovered a fifth primary taste, a savoury taste called umami. And now, researchers believe they have even found a sixth primary taste, and this may well affect the way in which we think about our food.

We experience the five distinct tastes because they react with our taste buds, the sensory organs in our mouths that allow us to distinguish between different tastes. There are thousands of these taste buds on the human tongue and all around the inside of our mouths. So, how we experience a mouthful of food really does depend on how the chemicals in the food affect our taste buds. Scientists now believe that fat may affect our taste buds in a similar way to other tastes, such as sour and sweet. We've known for some time that taste buds recognise fat. Scientists have, therefore, speculated that fat may produce a taste of its own which is distinguishable from the five other primary tastes. **37** ______

The researchers conducted two experiments. **38** ______ In the first, participants were given liquids that had one of six different tastes: sweet, salty, sour, bitter, umami and fatty. They were then asked to sort them into groups, as they believed were necessary. The participants had little trouble identifying sweet, salty and sour as unique tastes, but, interestingly, they put the remaining three all together into a single, separate group.

The researchers then took things a stage further. **39** ______ In the next experiment, they only gave participants solutions containing the three remaining tastes, and this time the participants had no difficulty separating them into three distinct groups. 'It was really very telling,' said Mattes, one of the scientists. 'We already knew that people have a taste receptor for fatty acids; now we know that it's a distinguishable taste.'

Fat, as everyone experiences it, is made up of three fatty acids. The combination of the three gives fat the creaminess we associate with it. The kind of fat Mattes is talking about is actually only in one of those three fatty acids. It's the one that gives us the taste that is unique to fat. A primary taste can only be called that if it shares no characteristics with the other primary tastes. The fact that people can so easily recognise fat as a different kind of taste is evidence that it is another primary taste. When you eat a food that contains fat, you don't immediately perceive the taste produced by this particular fatty acid. **40** ______

As a taste on its own, fat is pretty unappealing. 'It's very harsh,' said Mattes. 'It doesn't taste good.' But then, neither do some of the other primary tastes, such as bitter or sour. However, when added to other ingredients, it contributes greatly to the appeal of food, as is the case when it is used in combination with cocoa beans to make chocolate, for example. Many things are unpleasant in isolation, in fact. **41** ______

The impact of Mattes' research could extend well beyond the reach of his lab, to what appears on our plates. **42** ______ 'Understanding this could have huge implications for the food industry,' he said. If food manufacturers begin to concentrate on the flavour of fat as well as the creamy texture of it in our mouths, our food might actually start to taste better.'

A Fat is a perfect example of this.

B There isn't a firm agreement about what characteristics are necessary.

C That's when a clear division surfaced.

D Now there's evidence that it does.

E But it's there, and it's distinct.

F And, more specifically, it may affect how it tastes.

G This was to find out whether fat could be another of the basic tastes.

Part 7

You are going to read an article in which four students talk about subjects they enjoyed studying at school. For questions **43–52**, choose from the people (**A–D**). The people may be chosen more than once.

Mark your answers **on the separate answer sheet**.

Which girl

was shown the appeal of a subject she hadn't previously considered?	**43**	
says that she has learnt to solve complicated problems effectively?	**44**	
appreciates that a subject is of interest to diverse groups of people?	**45**	
sometimes received negative comments about her work?	**46**	
hid her true feelings about what her future might hold?	**47**	
felt that she had little chance of achieving an ambition?	**48**	
was frustrated at a lack of opportunity to be creative?	**49**	
enjoyed observing practical demonstrations in the subject?	**50**	
can understand why she was discouraged from studying something?	**51**	
found that potentially dull material was brought to life?	**52**	

Favourite subjects

A Tamsin

My Latin and Greek teacher taught me an invaluable lesson – that if you can excel at only one thing, then exploit that fully. I was a bit bored at school, and although I pretended otherwise, I was actually rather concerned about what lay ahead when I eventually left. But for some reason I'd always had an interest in the wonders of classical civilisation. The teacher loved her subject, and though she didn't hold back on the criticism when I messed up, she praised me to the skies when I met her expectations. She made what could simply have been dusty, dry books relevant to the modern world. I became fascinated not only with understanding the way society works, but also what makes people tick and how they deal with problems in life – and that's exactly what the ancient Greek tragedies are all about. And now I'm studying all this at university, and I feel really mentally stimulated.

B Bella

I liked art at school and, at one point, I even thought about studying it at university. But my parents put an end to that idea, as they said the subject wasn't appropriate for someone with my academic ability. Looking back I can see their point, but I felt I really needed some sort of outlet for my artistic ideas. Then, I discovered poetry, thanks to an outstanding teacher, who opened my eyes to the power of words, and encouraged me to go on to study English literature at university, which I'm now doing. And recently, I've taken to visiting museums, at quiet times, when the lack of bustling crowds means that you can stare at a painting or sculpture for as long as you want. Those visits are really important to me, and on my course I find I'm benefitting from the extra dimension that art brings to my reasoning.

C Karina

When I was at school, I always wanted to become a writer of some kind, although it somehow just felt hopelessly unrealistic. But I read an enormous amount, and loved playing around with words, so English literature was at the top of my list of favourite subjects. And studying it has given me more than I could ever have imagined. I've come to understand that modern works can be read for their underlying meaning rather than just the simple beauty of their prose. Now I've grasped that, the subject has become transformed for me into something with even greater significance. I realise that literature connects with people's lives and speaks to people no matter what their background might be. And, for me, the thrill of uncovering the hidden messages contained in a work of literature hasn't diminished in any way.

D Holly

At school, I always found the laws of physics fascinating to study, and memorable to see in action in classroom experiments. Luckily I was really good at maths, so the calculations we had to do weren't as taxing to me as they were to other students. And I got really carried away with experimenting – I made a device to measure magnetic fields with lasers. Physics is the study of the basic rules governing the universe, and the impact they have on our everyday lives. Studying it has helped me to develop a more analytical approach to any issue I have to deal with. It's given me the confidence to break down tricky tasks into manageable parts. And that has been really beneficial to me in my physics course at university.

WRITING (1 hour 20 minutes)

Part 1

You **must** answer this question. Write your answer in **140–190** words in an appropriate style **on the separate answer sheet**.

---

1 In your English class you have been talking about the opportunities teenagers have. Now your English teacher has asked you to write an essay for homework.

Write your essay using **all** the notes and giving reasons for your point of view.

'Young people nowadays have many more opportunities than young people had in the past.' Do you agree?

Notes

Write about:

1. education
2. travel
3. .... (your own idea)

Part 2

Write an answer to one of the questions **2–4** in this part. Write your answer in **140–190** words in an appropriate style **on the separate answer sheet**. Put the question number in the box at the top of the answer sheet.

---

2 You have seen this announcement in an English-language magazine for teenagers:

> *Stories wanted*
>
> We are looking for stories for our new English-language magazine for teenagers. Your story must **begin** with this sentence:
>
> *This was our first camping trip and we were really excited.*
>
> Your story must include:
>
> - a storm
> - a problem

Write your **story**.

3 You see this notice in an international magazine for teenagers:

> *Articles wanted*
>
> **School Rules!**
>
> Which rules at your school do you agree with and which ones do you think are unfair?
>
> Why is it important for students to have rules at school?
>
> The best articles will be published next month.

Write your **article**.

4 You recently saw this notice on a shopping website:

> *Reviews wanted*
>
> **Games and Toy Shops**
>
> Do you know a good shop which sells games or toys? If so, write us a review describing the shop and what it sells. Explain why the shop is a particularly good place to buy games or toys.
>
> The best reviews will be published next month.

Write your **review**.

LISTENING (approximately 40 minutes)

Part 1

You will hear people talking in eight different situations.

For questions **1–8**, choose the best answer (**A**, **B** or **C**).

---

1 You hear part of an interview with a tennis player after a match.

How does she feel?

A disappointed to have been injured

B grateful for the help she's received

C impressed by her opponent's performance

2 You hear two friends talking about a comedy show they went to see.

What do they agree about?

A how unsuitable the venue was

B how enthusiastic the audience was

C how original the comedian's humour was

3 You hear part of a radio phone-in programme about cycling in cities.

What is the caller doing?

A criticising the lack of cycling facilities

B encouraging people to take up cycling

C complaining about the way cyclists behave

4 You hear two friends discussing an article about junk food.

What does the girl suggest about it?

A It won't appeal to many people she knows.

B It contains information that is inaccurate.

C It is unlikely to affect the way she lives.

5 You hear a teacher talking about a large picture her students are painting to be displayed.

Why does the teacher want her students to paint the picture?

A to improve their ability to work as a team

B to make them aware of art in the area

C to encourage them to think creatively

6 You hear a boy telling a friend about a trip he went on with his father.

What does he say about it?

A He appreciated his father's attempts to please him.

B He was confident of his father's ability to organise things.

C He admired his father's knowledge of other places.

7 You hear a girl talking about a science experiment at her school.

She says that the experiment

A didn't work as well as intended.

B had an unexpected consequence.

C demonstrated an important scientific principle.

8 You hear two friends discussing an experiment into the effects of spending time in space.

What do they both think about it?

A They're interested to learn more.

B They admire the participants' courage.

C They'd be reluctant to do something similar.

Part 2

You will hear an interview with a boy called Luke Tyler, who took part in a desert marathon race. For questions **9–18**, complete the sentences with a word or short phrase.

Desert marathon race

The **(9)** .... for competitors are the same each year.

In his backpack, Luke made sure he put a **(10)** .... that didn't weigh very much.

When getting ready for the race, Luke thinks that his **(11)** .... helped him more than anything else.

Before the race, Luke was nervous about the danger of **(12)** .... in the desert.

Luke thinks he should have eaten more **(13)** .... during the marathon.

The runners stopped at places known as **(14)** .... where they could have a short rest.

Luke is pleased that he chose the right sort of **(15)** .... for the race.

Luke says the **(16)** .... were the most memorable things he saw in the desert.

Luke threw away some **(17)** .... which were items he didn't need.

Luke mentions that there were **(18)** .... which carried some larger items needed for overnight stops.

Part 3

You will hear five short extracts in which teenagers are talking about what's called a survival course, where they learnt the skills you need to live in a forest. For questions **19–23**, choose from the list **(A–H)** how each speaker felt during the course. Use the letters only once. There are three extra letters which you do not need to use.

A irritated by other students' behaviour

B concerned about the possibility of falling ill

C enthusiastic about working in a team

D frustrated by the time it took to do something

E impressed by someone's ability

F disappointed to miss out on something

G grateful for the opportunity to do something unusual

H surprised by how challenging some of the tasks were

Speaker 1		**19**
Speaker 2		**20**
Speaker 3		**21**
Speaker 4		**22**
Speaker 5		**23**

Part 4

You will hear an interview with a man called Danny Taylor, who is a record producer with his own recording studio. For questions **24–30**, choose the best answer (**A**, **B** or **C**).

---

24 Why did Danny decide to start his recording studio?

A He had difficulty finding a job in the music industry.

B He was keen to work with a variety of musicians.

C He wanted to record more of his own music.

25 When asked about the way his studio has developed, Danny says he's

A proud of the reputation he's built up.

B relieved that his business has kept going so long.

C frustrated about having to do certain kinds of work.

26 What does Danny say about the location of his studio?

A It differs from many other studios.

B It affects the style of music made there.

C It puts off younger bands and musicians.

27 What does Danny say about the behaviour of bands he works with?

A The way they interact is not reflected in their music.

B The stress involved in recording often leads to arguments.

C The image presented in the media is usually misleading.

28 What does Danny find hardest about his work?

A criticising musicians who lack talent

B deciding which bands he wants to work with

C dealing with the demands of well-known musicians

29 What does Danny think is his greatest strength as a music producer?

A his skill at helping inexperienced musicians improve

B his ability to make a song sound original

C his awareness of what will sell well

30 What advice does Danny offer people interested in becoming music producers?

A Remember that music production requires a great deal of commitment.

B Keep up-to-date with the latest music production technology.

C Find a course with links to the music industry.

SPEAKING (14 minutes)

You take the Speaking test with another candidate (possibly two candidates), referred to here as your partner. There are two examiners. One will speak to you and your partner and the other will be listening. Both examiners will award marks.

Part 1 (2 minutes (3 minutes for groups of three))

The examiner asks you and your partner questions about yourselves. You may be asked about things like 'your home town', 'your interests', 'your career plans', etc.

Part 2 (4 minutes (6 minutes for part three))

The examiner gives you two photographs and asks you to talk about them for one minute. The examiner then asks your partner a question about your photographs and your partner responds briefly.

Then the examiner gives your partner two different photographs. Your partner talks about these photographs for one minute. This time the examiner asks you a question about your partner's photographs and you respond briefly.

Part 3 (4 minutes (5 minutes for groups of three))

The examiner asks you and your partner to talk together. They give you a task to look at so you can think about and discuss an idea, giving reasons for your opinion. For example, you may be asked to think about some changes in the world, or about spending free time with your family. After you have discussed the task for about two minutes with your partner, the examiner will ask you a follow-up question, which you should discuss for a further minute.

Part 4 (4 minutes (6 minutes for groups of three))

The examiner asks some further questions, which leads to a more general discussion of what you have talked about in Part 3. You may comment on your partner's answers if you wish.

Test 4

READING AND USE OF ENGLISH (1 hour 15 minutes)

Part 1

For questions **1–8**, read the text below and decide which answer (**A**, **B**, **C** or **D**) best fits each gap. There is an example at the beginning (**0**).

Mark your answers **on the separate answer sheet.**

Example:

0 **A** careless **B** casual **C** comfortable **D** chance

Computer games may be good for the brain!

Playing computer games is no longer just a **(0)** .... pastime. Researchers are therefore increasingly curious to discover whether it **(1)** .... learning and, if so, how. A recent study has **(2)** .... that gamers are more efficient at visual task learning (learning by watching), than non-gamers.

In the study, keen gamers were compared with people who had rarely, if **(3)** .... , played video games. Each group was trained in two visual tasks. Improving visual learning takes time; usually, if a second task is **(4)** .... before the brain has had a chance to learn how to do the first one, it results in a decline in performance. So the following day, the participants were asked to **(5)** .... the same tasks again. The frequent gamers showed great **(6)** .... in both tasks, but the non-gamers' performance on the first task became worse. The scientists are not sure why this is the **(7)** .... but believe the learning process may be speeded up by the vast amount of visual training frequent gamers are **(8)** .... to over the years.

1	**A**	adapts	**B**	affects	**C**	relates	**D**	concerns
2	**A**	established	**B**	supposed	**C**	presented	**D**	examined
3	**A**	even	**B**	hardly	**C**	ever	**D**	yet
4	**A**	developed	**B**	inserted	**C**	raised	**D**	introduced
5	**A**	take up	**B**	carry out	**C**	get over	**D**	put forward
6	**A**	increase	**B**	advance	**C**	development	**D**	progress
7	**A**	case	**B**	fact	**C**	circumstance	**D**	position
8	**A**	supplied	**B**	provided	**C**	exposed	**D**	revealed

Part 2

For questions **9–16**, read the text below and think of the word which best fits each gap. Use only **one** word in each gap. There is an example at the beginning (**0**).

Write your answers **IN CAPITAL LETTERS on the separate answer sheet.**

Example:	**0**	A

The Crystal Palace dinosaurs

The Crystal Palace dinosaurs are **(0)** .... collection of over 30 statues. They stand proudly overlooking a park in the London suburb of the same name. The park and dinosaur displays are open to the public and are free to visit. School groups frequently go and look at the dinosaurs, but **(9)** .... help preserve them, the statues are viewed from a distance and cannot **(10)** .... climbed. Created in around 1854, they were the first ever attempt anywhere in the world to represent dinosaurs as full-scale, three-dimensional, active creatures.

Some of the statues are dramatically different when **(11)** .... comes to comparing them with modern interpretations of dinosaurs. Which experts in the 1850s decided what the statues should look **(12)** .... is a subject of historical debate. However, research clearly shows that experts at the time **(13)** .... different interpretations of the dinosaurs, and these differences of opinion **(14)** .... reflected in the statues currently **(15)** .... display at Crystal Palace. The way in **(16)** .... these various interpretations have evolved demonstrates how scientific ideas often develop.

Part 3

For questions **17–24**, read the text below. Use the word given in capitals at the end of some of the lines to form a word that fits in the gap **in the same line**. There is an example at the beginning (**0**).

Write your answers **IN CAPITAL LETTERS on the separate answer sheet.**

Example: | **0** | *THOUGHT* |

Food miles

Have you ever given any **(0)** .... to how far your food has	**THINK**
travelled before it arrives at your local shop? You might be	
surprised at the distance, or number of 'food miles' involved. And	
this isn't an easy **(17)** .... to make. However, some people are	**CALCULATE**
becoming **(18)** .... concerned that ignoring the issue of food	**INCREASE**
miles when shopping is **(19)** .... and can have a negative	**RESPONSIBLE**
impact on the environment. Buying food that has been **(20)**	**PRODUCT**
locally may appear to be the answer, but there are other factors	
to take into **(21)** .... For example, in the UK it may be more	**CONSIDER**
(22) .... friendly to import tomatoes rather than grow them, because	**ENVIRONMENT**
the **(23)** .... British weather can mean that a lot of electricity	**PREDICT**
is needed to heat greenhouses. It's difficult to know what the best	
solution is, but a good first step might be for **(24)** .... to do more of	**CONSUME**
their shopping in markets, where food tends to have less packaging.	

Part 4

For questions **25–30**, complete the second sentence so that it has a similar meaning to the first sentence, using the word given. **Do not change the word given**. You must use between **two** and **five** words, including the word given. Here is an example (**0**).

Example:

0 Prizes are given out when the school year finishes.

PLACE

Prize-giving .... end of the school year.

The gap can be filled by the words 'takes place at the', so you write:

Example:	**0**	*TAKES PLACE AT THE*

Write **only** the missing words **IN CAPITAL LETTERS on the separate answer sheet.**

---

25 It hasn't stopped raining all day so I can't go out!

WOULD

I .... raining so I could go out!

26 If chemistry is what you want to study next year, don't let your friends discourage you.

PUT

Don't let your friends .... studying chemistry next year, if that's what you want to do.

27 As far as I know, Mary's not back from holiday until next week.

BEST

To .... knowledge, Mary's not back from holiday until next week.

28 Membership fees for the after-school football club should be reduced significantly.

SIGNIFICANT

There needs .... in membership fees for the after-school football club.

29 The door was stuck and I couldn't open it, despite trying really hard.

MATTER

The door was stuck and I couldn't open it, ... tried.

30 How did Michael persuade you to help him with his project?

TALK

How did Michael .... him with his project?

Part 5

You are going to read an article about a teenager who is talking about long family car journeys. For questions **31–36**, choose the answer (**A**, **B**, **C** or **D**) which you think fits best according to the text.

Mark your answers **on the separate answer sheet**.

Family road trips

By Ben Robinson, aged 16

I'm just going to say this once, for the record: when you're travelling by car somewhere with your family, even when you're six years old, the chances are you know full well that you're not 'there yet,' even as you're asking over and over 'Are we there yet?' And anyway, the truth of the matter is, once you get there it's not 'there' anymore, is it? It's 'here'. So if you really think there's a chance that you're 'there' yet, you should be asking 'Are we *here* yet?' And I'm pretty sure there's no one who wishes they were 'there yet' more than the mums and dads fielding that question over and over every single long car trip.

I mean, seriously – what are us kids complaining about? Just think about it. Wouldn't you prefer to be lounging in the back seat, with nothing being demanded of you? So you watch endless DVDs that you've never seemed to get round to seeing before, listen to music, perhaps indulge in a few of the puzzles you've had for ages but not done, as the scenic vistas roll on by endlessly outside the window.

And acting as co-pilot in the passenger seat, map in hand, there'll be mum or dad, whose function is to dole out juice boxes, and cookies, or to adjust the radio station and temperature to whatever is requested – in short, to keep it all running smoothly and be the on-the-road concierge! Are we there yet? I hope not.

That is, of course, until someone in the car does something unthinkable – in my case generally my younger brother, Tim. Something like … putting his foot on my side of the seat. What? He can't do that! So I put my foot on his side. And then it's his other foot, and then a hand, and next thing you know he's hurled his whole body over into my space and a fight has erupted. And the driver and co-pilot start reaching back and separating us as the car accelerates and swerves. They heatedly tell the younger sibling off, saying he should stay in his own seat and keep his hands to himself. This restores civility for a while. And the scenic wonders, steeped in history, continue rolling by.

And pretty soon after that, I'm trying to read, and suddenly I feel something – a draught blowing across my arm. But the car's not going that fast and the window's not even open. So where's it coming from? My vengeful sibling is in the next seat, discreetly but purposefully channeling his breath onto me. He's on his side, perfectly legitimately, not touching me – so he's got me on a technicality. Just breathing. What's the problem with that? The anger escalates. Tim gets yelled at, there's more swerving. Then slowly the madness subsides again – for now.

Over the years, Dad's developed strategies for dealing with us kids on the back seat. For example, his response to the question 'Are we there yet?' has frequently been, 'Yup. We're here. Get out of the car.'

'But Dad. We're still on the highway, going 70 miles an hour.'

'Oh, well, then maybe we're not there yet.' That kept everyone quiet for a while. Mind you, you can tell when you're finally 'there' when you see the grown-ups tumble out of the car and go as far away as they can from the kids who've tormented them for all those hours. So once and for all, please note: if mum and dad are still near enough to answer your question, then the answer is: no. You're not there yet.

31 What is Ben doing in the first paragraph?

A explaining his poor behaviour when travelling
B revealing his dislike of lengthy car journeys
C giving an example of a source of annoyance on trips
D describing a strategy to make journeys pass quickly

32 What is Ben's attitude to the activities he does during the journey?

A He regards them as a bit of a waste of time.
B He regrets that they distract him from the views outside.
C He admits they are not ones he would enjoy doing at home.
D He takes advantage of being free from other obligations.

33 How does Ben behave towards his younger brother Tim during a journey?

A He overreacts to trivial things that Tim does.
B He deliberately encourages Tim to continue to fight.
C He places the blame for any arguments on Tim.
D He tricks Tim into misbehaving.

34 What does 'This' refer to in line 43?

A the speed of the car
B the adults' response
C the fight
D Tim's behaviour

35 What does 'he's got me on a technicality' mean in lines 53 and 54?

A He has taken pleasure in Ben's discomfort.
B He has used the rules to defeat Ben.
C He has managed to spoil Ben's journey.
D He has realised what has annoyed Ben.

36 In the final paragraph, Ben reveals his

A lack of understanding of his dad's sense of humour.
B sympathy for what his parents have endured.
C concern that he has pushed his parents too far.
D resentment at his parents' wish to distance themselves.

Part 6

You are going to read a newspaper article about listening to birdsong. Six sentences have been removed from the article. Choose from the sentences **A–G** the one which fits each gap (**37–42**). There is one extra sentence which you do not need to use.

Mark your answers **on the separate answer sheet.**

The importance of birdsong

Do you enjoy listening to birdsong and, if so, how often do you *really* listen to it? One of the pleasures I share with my grandfather is a love of birds, and in particular listening to their different songs. Some people who hear a bird singing say 'That sounds lovely', without feeling any need to identify the bird in question. Others, including dedicated bird-watchers, will hear the song and immediately set about trying to identify the bird. **37** ____ After all, the next interesting species is sure to turn up soon. My grandfather takes yet another approach.

Recently we made a plan. We decided that once a week or so, we'd go down to the wetlands near where we live, take a hot drink and sit and listen to a species of bird called the sedge warbler. Out on empty wetlands, you can't help but hear these creatures. We don't concern ourselves with whether they're male or female, or what exactly they're doing. **38** ____ Although they may not sing as beautifully as some other birds, they're still worth paying attention to.

In fact, if you look at a scientific analysis of their song, you find that they sing for an entire minute without stopping, and in that time, they will utter around 300 syllables. **39** ____ They will introduce up to ten new syllables in that section. And some analysts say that the music they make is so intricate that they never sing the same song twice.

However, actually being able to hear birdsong is becoming more of a challenge these days as the air is increasingly filled with the noise of machines and traffic. **40** ____ But then we also risk missing natural sounds, and those, it seems, are important for our well-being. Studies have shown that exposure to white noise negatively affects our concentration and stress levels.

Listening to birdsong is the perfect antidote. Recent research has shown what many of us have always thought. **41** ____ There's also evidence that it can lead to a reduction in anxiety levels, particularly useful in hospital environments, for example. These benefits have also been recognised in locations such as airports. One airport has started to play birdsong to passengers in its quiet lounge, where people can unwind before flights, and so far, feedback has been very positive.

Birdsong is also a great reminder that despite human activity, much of which can severely affect their habitats, there are entire communities of birds that are thriving – and living independently alongside us. As birds go about their daily business of laying eggs, raising chicks and finding food, they aren't concerned with us in the least. We may be the centre of our own worlds, but we are most certainly not the centre of theirs. **42** ____ Indeed, seeing the world from a non-human perspective helps us to reconnect with nature and enables us to see the bigger picture.

A It provides physical relaxation as well as mental stimulation.

B The objective is rather to listen to the song as another example of how amazing nature can be.

C It can be a key indicator of the health of the bird population.

D The only solution is to wear headphones and block it all out.

E The middle of the song is the most complex.

F That is something we should be more aware of.

G Having done so to their satisfaction, they'll move on.

Part 7

You are going to read an article about some young film directors. For questions **43–52**, choose from the people (**A–D**). The people may be chosen more than once.

Mark your answers **on the separate answer sheet.**

Which person

describes the opportunity they were given to analyse challenging films?	**43**
admits their approach wasn't typical of the way new directors tend to behave?	**44**
believes that it is necessary to change the subject matter of their films regularly?	**45**
mentions the challenging environment they had to work in?	**46**
says that they don't want to criticise filmmakers in a different working environment?	**47**
admits they had difficulty mastering one skill required for their work?	**48**
describes a technique that they use to create a particular atmosphere in their films?	**49**
explains how they aren't limited by certain demands that other filmmakers have to meet?	**50**
enjoys writing about complex personalities that may not be easy to like?	**51**
mentions how the actors need to feel committed to what they are doing?	**52**

Young film di ectors

A **Laurence Yuen**

My main task is to come up with a narrative that everyone finds engaging. It's all down to the quality of that story because, if a director isn't working in Hollywood or somewhere like that, there might not be the budget to pay the cast what they deserve. This means they all need to believe passionately in the story that's being told and want to come to work every day despite the lack of financial reward. I'd never knock people employed by the big studios because some fantastic films are made there, but independent filmmakers like me have greater freedom, so we can tell more unusual stories without worrying too much about the need to make money or please huge audiences. For example, I like creating characters that are different from what you might typically see in big Hollywood movies and which don't always conform to stereotypes.

B **Daisy Morgan**

I didn't start out with an interest in making animated films, but I gradually realised there was potential in that field. I struggled initially and it took me a good six months to get the hang of it. When most directors make their first animated feature film, they keep things fairly modest. I didn't scale back or limit my ambition even though we ended up having to do the filming in a confined space – it was really cramped. A vital part of the process of writing a film is finding someone to do it with – someone who on a basic level you're compatible with, but doesn't have exactly the same way of doing things. What almost defeated me was the writing, actually. My first few drafts were too long and needed a huge amount of editing, which was hard to take because very promising material had to be cut.

C **Antonio Rossi**

As a teenager, I'd watch teen movies and then I'd get fed up and, with my parents' encouragement, would watch some of their movies as well and discuss them in detail. This exposed me to complex, sophisticated filmmaking at an early age. Some directors choose to limit themselves to particular themes because it brings them success and popularity. But I try to shake things up when I can – it's the only way to improve, I think. Attending film festivals is a great way of getting direct audience feedback on your work, but having said that, I try not to worry too much if people react negatively towards my films. If I do that, then it starts to block my creativity. I'd love to write a comedy and I thought at one time it might be an easy option. It's not difficult to write what you personally find funny, but trying to write something that everyone else will find equally amusing is a different thing completely.

D **Anna Svensson**

I prefer writing and directing drama because it gives me the opportunity to create characters full of contradictions – characters that audiences won't necessarily warm to. I often include scenes without dialogue, which adds to the tension and suspense. I love the opportunity to create strong emotional responses in people, particularly by unexpectedly changing the way the viewer feels about a character. Getting hold of the best cameras and lighting is a challenge when you haven't got a huge budget. Trying to decide on what camera to use is sometimes a bit tricky too. We've found that with an inexperienced cast bigger cameras can be off-putting and intrusive. Several top directors may have influenced my work, and I don't think you can hide that from anyone. In the early days I may have stolen some ideas from them, but I didn't see that I was doing it. Even so, it's a bit embarrassing when I look back at my first attempts at filmmaking.

WRITING (1 hour 20 minutes)

Part 1

You **must** answer this question. Write your answer in **140–190** words in an appropriate style on **the separate answer sheet**.

---

1 In your English class you have been talking about schools. Now your English teacher has asked you to write an essay for homework.

Write your essay using **all** the notes and giving reasons for your point of view.

Some people say that schools will be very different in the future.

What do you think?

Notes

Write about:

1. the teachers
2. the subjects
3. .... (your own idea)

Part 2

Write an answer to **one** of the questions **2–4** in this part. Write your answer in **140–190** words in an appropriate style **on the separate answer sheet**. Put the question number in the box at the top of the answer sheet.

---

2 You see this announcement in an international e-magazine for teenagers:

> *Articles wanted*
>
> **The Weather!**
>
> What is your favourite kind of weather and what kind of weather do you hate? Why? What effect does different weather have on your mood?
>
> The best articles will appear online next week.

Write your **article**.

3 You recently saw this notice in an English magazine:

> *Reviews wanted*
>
> **Family-friendly restaurants**
>
> Do you know a restaurant which is especially good for families with children of different ages? If so, write a review describing the restaurant, explaining what kind of food it serves and saying why it is a good restaurant for the whole family.
>
> We will post the best reviews on our website.

Write your **review**.

4 You have received this email from your English friend, Arthur:

> Hi!
>
> My older brother, Stan, is going to your country next year to study. He wants to find out if there are any customs or traditions he should know about. Also, he's not sure whether to live in an apartment on his own or to live with a local family. Which would be best and why?
>
> Thanks
>
> Arthur

Write your **email**.

LISTENING (approximately 40 minutes)

Part 1

You will hear people talking in eight different situations.

For questions **1–8**, choose the best answer (**A**, **B** or **C**).

---

1 You hear two friends talking about a pop band they saw on TV.

What surprised them both about the band members?

A the wide range of ages

B their level of popularity

C the quality of their voices

2 You hear part of an interview with a scientist.

What is he doing?

A explaining why some research has produced unclear results

B criticising the reluctance of some schools to co-operate with him

C pointing out the possible value of making some controversial changes

3 You hear a teacher talking to a student about doing homework.

What advice does she give?

A Take regular short breaks.

B Deal with the difficult things first.

C Cut down on free-time activities.

4 You hear a football fan talking about his team.

He blames their poor results on

A their struggle to maintain energy levels.

B their poor organisation on the pitch.

C their lack of belief in themselves.

5 You hear a film critic talking about a film for teenagers.

What does she say about it?

A She was impressed by the special effects.

B It was better than the book it was based on.

C The actor who played the leading role performed well.

6 You hear two teenagers discussing a visit to a zoo.

They agree that zoos

A attract tourists in imaginative ways.

B can succeed in educating people.

C play a valuable role in conservation.

7 You hear a young professional ballet dancer talking about performing.

What does she say about being on stage?

A She tries to forget any critical comments she's heard.

B She succeeds by pretending to be confident.

C She reveals a very different side of herself.

8 You hear a teacher talking about the history of the refrigerator.

What does he say about it?

A Its introduction caused a great deal of excitement.

B Its potential wasn't recognised for some time.

C Its long-term significance has been overestimated.

Part 2

You will hear a man called Jack Morton talking about his job as a windsurfing instructor. For questions **9–18**, complete the sentences with a word or short phrase.

Jack Morton – windsurfing instructo

Jack's first experience of work was as a **(9)** ....

The name of the first watersports company that Jack worked for was

(10) ....

What particularly attracts Jack to windsurfing is the **(11)** .... involved.

Jack most enjoys the moment when his beginners learn to **(12)** ....

on the board successfully.

Jack uses the word **(13)** .... to describe how some learners feel

when they succeed.

Jack explains that getting enough **(14)** .... is more important than

anything else when learning to windsurf.

Jack feels that the **(15)** .... is something many windsurfers fail to

think carefully about.

Jack mentions parking a car to explain that people should give each other

(16) .... when windsurfing.

The fact that he is **(17)** .... has earned Jack praise from his employer.

Jack says that **(18)** .... as well as promotional skills are becoming

more important in watersports careers.

Part 3

You will hear five short extracts in which teenagers are remembering the day they met their best friend for the first time. For questions **19–23**, choose from the list (**A–H**) how each speaker felt on that day. Use the letters only once. There are three extra letters which you do not need to use.

A disappointed by something the friend said

B pleased to find they shared an interest

C embarrassed by a misunderstanding

D surprised that they hadn't met previously

E happy about a suggestion the friend made

F amused by something they saw together

G nervous about what they had to do together

H curious about the friend's experiences

Speaker 1		**19**
Speaker 2		**20**
Speaker 3		**21**
Speaker 4		**22**
Speaker 5		**23**

Part 4

You will hear an interview with a young artist called Martin Gold, who is learning how to draw the cartoon stories that appear in magazines. For questions **24–30**, choose the best answer (**A**, **B** or **C**).

---

24 What attracted Martin to drawing cartoons?

A his wish to demonstrate his originality

B his fascination with reading comics

C his interest in the techniques involved

25 Martin's school teacher reacted to his choice of career by warning him that

A she couldn't help him to get work experience.

B it would be very hard to find a secure job.

C he might need to consider an alternative to it.

26 Martin continued to follow his ambition because of

A the surprising popularity of his artwork.

B the confidence he had in his own abilities.

C the encouraging responses he'd received from magazines.

27 How did visiting Barcelona help Martin?

A He received help developing his drawing techniques.

B He felt inspired by his experiences there.

C He realised what he really liked about art.

28 By using a different kind of ink for drawing his cartoons, Martin

A increased the amount he was able to produce.

B included a greater degree of detail.

C extended the range of images he can draw.

29 How does Martin feel about his work as a 'ghost artist'?

A It's proving a less valuable experience than he'd hoped.

B It's preventing him from developing his own cartoons.

C It isn't regular enough for him to rely on financially.

30 Martin thinks that he might have problems working as a cartoonist because of

A his tendency to take on too many challenges.

B his reluctance to accept advice from others.

C his disorganised approach to his work.

SPEAKING (14 minutes)

You take the Speaking test with another candidate (possibly two candidates), referred to here as your partner. There are two examiners. One will speak to you and your partner and the other will be listening. Both examiners will award marks.

Part 1 (2 minutes (3 minutes for groups of three))

The examiner asks you and your partner questions about yourselves. You may be asked about things like 'your home town', 'your interests', 'your career plans', etc.

Part 2 (4 minutes (6 minutes for groups of three))

The examiner gives you two photographs and asks you to talk about them for one minute.
The examiner then asks your partner a question about your photographs and your partner responds briefly.
Then the examiner gives your partner two different photographs. Your partner talks about these photographs for one minute. This time the examiner asks you a question about your partner's photographs and you respond briefly.

Part 3 (4 minutes (5 minutes for groups of three))

The examiner asks you and your partner to talk together. They give you a task to look at so you can think about and discuss an idea, giving reasons for your opinion. For example, you may be asked to think about some changes in the world, or about spending free time with your family. After you have discussed the task for about two minutes with your partner, the examiner will ask you a follow-up question, which you should discuss for a further minute.

Part 4 (4 minutes (6 minutes for groups of three))

The examiner asks some further questions, which leads to a more general discussion of what you have talked about in Part 3. You may comment on your partner's answers if you wish.

Frames for the Speaking test

Test 1

Note: In the examination, there will be both an assessor and an interlocutor in the room. The visual material for **Test 1** appears on pages C1 and C2 (Part 2), and C3 (Part 3).

Part 1 2 minutes (3 minutes for groups of three)

Interlocutor: Good morning/afternoon/evening. My name is .... and this is my colleague ....
And your names are?
Can I have your mark sheets, please? Thank you.

- Where are you from, *(Candidate A)*?
- And you, *(Candidate B)*?

First, we'd like to know something about you.

Select one or more questions from any of the following categories, as appropriate.

Habits and routines
- Do you like to be busy every day? (Why? / Why not?)
- What sport do you enjoy playing? (Why do you like doing that?)
- Do you enjoy watching TV? (What's your favourite programme?) (Why do you like it?)
- Do you ever meet your friends in the evenings after school? (What do you do together?)

The weekend
- Do you prefer to spend time with your family or with your friends at the weekend? (Why?)
- Are there a lot of interesting things to do in your town at the weekend? (What do you do there?)
- Do you often have to do homework at the weekend? (How do you feel about that?)
- Can you tell us something about what you're planning to do next weekend?

The future
- What are you going to do after school today? (Why?)
- What would you like to do for your next birthday? (Why?)
- Is there something you'd like to learn in the future? (What would you like to learn?) (Why?)
- What would you like to do when you leave school? (Why?)

Part 2 4 minutes (6 minutes for groups of three)

After school clubs
Taking photographs

Interlocutor: In this part of the test, I'm going to give each of you two photographs. I'd like you to talk about your photographs on your own for about a minute, and also to answer a question about your partner's photographs.

(Candidate A), it's your turn first. Here are your photographs. They show people doing activities in after school clubs.

Indicate pictures 1A and 1B on page C1 to Candidate A.

I'd like you to compare the photographs, and say what you think the people are enjoying about doing these activities in after school clubs.

All right?

Candidate A: [*1 minute*]

Interlocutor: Thank you.

(Candidate B), which of these activities would you prefer to do? (Why?)

Candidate B: [*Approximately 30 seconds*]

Interlocutor: Thank you.

Now, *(Candidate B)*, here are your photographs. They show people taking photographs in different situations.

Indicate pictures 1C and 1D on page C2 to Candidate B.

I'd like you to compare the photographs, and say why you think the people have decided to take photographs in these situations.

All right?

Candidate B: [*1 minute*]

Interlocutor: Thank you.

(Candidate A), do you enjoy taking photographs? (Why?)

Candidate A: [*Approximately 30 seconds*]

Interlocutor: Thank you.

Parts 3 and 4

Helping children with homework

Part 3 4 minutes (5 minutes for groups of three)

Interlocutor: Now, I'd like you to talk about something together for about two minutes. [*3 minutes for groups of three*]

Some parents help children with their homework, and other parents don't. Here are some things they think about and a question for you to discuss. First you have some time to look at the task.

Indicate the visual 1E on page C3 to the candidates. Allow 15 seconds.

Now, talk to each other about whether you think parents should help children with their homework.

Candidates: [*2 minutes / 3 minutes for groups of three*]

Interlocutor: Thank you. Now you have about a minute to decide what you think is the best reason for parents to help children with their homework.

Candidates: [*1 minute*]

Interlocutor: Thank you.

Part 4 4 minutes (6 minutes for groups of three)

Interlocutor: *Use the following questions, in order, as appropriate:*

- Do your parents give you a lot of help with your homework? (What do they help with?)
- Some people say that children shouldn't do any homework during the school week. Do you agree? (Why? / Why not?)
- Do you think the school day should be longer so that students don't have to do work at home? (Why? / Why not?)
- Some people say that homework isn't a good thing for children because they stay up too late doing it. What do you think?
- Do you think it would be a good idea for students to do homework online so that the teachers can see what they've done? (Why? / Why not?)
- Do you think it's true that giving children prizes is the best way to encourage them to work harder? (Why? / Why not?)

Thank you. That is the end of the test.

Select any of the following prompts, as appropriate:

- What do you think?
- Do you agree?
- And you?

Test 2

Note: In the examination, there will be both an assessor and an interlocutor in the room.
The visual material for **Test 2** appears on pages C4 and C5 (Part 2), and C6 (Part 3).

Part 1 2 minutes (3 minutes for groups of three)

Interlocutor: Good morning/afternoon/evening. My name is .... and this is my colleague ....
And your names are?
Can I have your mark sheets, please? Thank you.

- Where are you from, *(Candidate A)*?
- And you, *(Candidate B)*?

First, we'd like to know something about you.

Select one or more questions from any of the following categories, as appropriate.

Habits and routines

- Do you like to be busy every day? (Why? / Why not?)
- What sport do you enjoy playing? (Why do you like doing that?)
- Do you enjoy watching TV? (What's your favourite programme?) (Why do you like it?)
- Do you ever meet your friends in the evenings after school? (What do you do together?)

The weekend

- Do you prefer to spend time with your family or with your friends at the weekend? (Why?)
- Are there a lot of interesting things to do in your town at the weekend? (What do you do there?)
- Do you often have to do homework at the weekend? (How do you feel about that?)
- Can you tell us something about what you're planning to do next weekend?

The future

- What are you going to do after school today? (Why?)
- What would you like to do for your next birthday? (Why?)
- Is there something you'd like to learn in the future? (What would you like to learn?) (Why?)
- What would you like to do when you leave school? (Why?)

Part 2 4 minutes (6 minutes for groups of three)

Listening carefully
Family holidays

Interlocutor: In this part of the test, I'm going to give each of you two photographs. I'd like you to talk about your photographs on your own for about a minute, and also to answer a question about your partner's photographs.

(Candidate A), it's your turn first. Here are your photographs. They show people listening carefully in different situations.

Indicate pictures 2A and 2B on page C4 to Candidate A.

I'd like you to compare the photographs, and say why you think the people are listening carefully in these situations.

All right?

Candidate A: [*1 minute*]

Interlocutor: Thank you.

(Candidate B), do you always listen carefully to your teachers? (Why?)

Candidate B: [*Approximately 30 seconds*]

Interlocutor: Thank you.

Now, *(Candidate B)*, here are your photographs. They show families spending their holidays in different places.

Indicate pictures 2C and 2D on page C5 to Candidate B.

I'd like you to compare the photographs, and say what you think the families are enjoying about spending their holidays in these places.

All right?

Candidate B: [*1 minute*]

Interlocutor: Thank you.

(Candidate A), do you enjoy spending time by the sea? (Why?)

Candidate A: [*Approximately 30 seconds*]

Interlocutor: Thank you.

Parts 3 and 4

Depending on the internet

Part 3 4 minutes (5 minutes for groups of three)

Interlocutor: Now, I'd like you to talk about something together for about two minutes. [*3 minutes for groups of three*]

Some people use the internet to find all the information they need, and others think this is not a good idea. Here are some things they think about and a question for you to discuss. First you have some time to look at the task.

Indicate the visual 2E on page C6 to the candidates.
Allow 15 seconds.

Now, talk to each other about whether it's a good idea for people to use the internet to find all the information they need.

Candidates: [*2 minutes / 3 minutes for groups of three*]

Interlocutor: Thank you. Now you have about a minute to decide what you think is the best reason for people not to depend on the internet for information.

Candidates: [*1 minute*]

Interlocutor: Thank you.

Part 4 4 minutes (6 minutes for groups of three)

Interlocutor: *Use the following questions, in order, as appropriate:*

- Do you and your friends always use the internet for doing your homework? (Why? / Why not?)
- Do you think parents should control how long their children spend online? (Why? / Why not?)
- Some people think we can learn more from watching television than from going online. What do you think?
- Should computers be part of every lesson at school? (Why? / Why not?)
- Sometimes people try to stay offline for a whole day. Do you think doing that's a good idea? (Why? / Why not?)
- A lot of people post pictures and information about what they're doing on the internet. Do you think that's a good thing to do? (Why do you say that?)

Select any of the following prompts, as appropriate:

- What do you think?
- Do you agree?
- And you?

Thank you. That is the end of the test.

Test 3

Note: In the examination, there will be both an assessor and an interlocutor in the room.
The visual material for **Test 3** appears on pages C7 and C8 (Part 2), and C9 (Part 3).

Part 1 2 minutes (3 minutes for groups of three)

Interlocutor: Good morning/afternoon/evening. My name is .... and this is my colleague ....
And your names are?
Can I have your mark sheets, please? Thank you.

- Where are you from, *(Candidate A)*?
- And you, *(Candidate B)*?

First, we'd like to know something about you.

Select one or more questions from any of the following categories, as appropriate.

Habits and routines
- Do you like to be busy every day? (Why? / Why not?)
- What sport do you enjoy playing? (Why do you like doing that?)
- Do you enjoy watching TV? (What's your favourite programme?) (Why do you like it?)
- Do you ever meet your friends in the evenings after school? (What do you do together?)

The weekend
- Do you prefer to spend time with your family or with your friends at the weekend? (Why?)
- Are there a lot of interesting things to do in your town at the weekend? (What do you do there?)
- Do you often have to do homework at the weekend? (How do you feel about that?)
- Can you tell us something about what you're planning to do next weekend?

The future
- What are you going to do after school today? (Why?)
- What would you like to do for your next birthday? (Why?)
- Is there something you'd like to learn in the future? (What would you like to learn?) (Why?)
- What would you like to do when you leave school? (Why?)

Part 2 4 minutes (6 minutes for groups of three)

Working together
Learning difficult things

Interlocutor: In this part of the test, I'm going to give each of you two photographs. I'd like you to talk about your photographs on your own for about a minute, and also to answer a question about your partner's photographs.

(Candidate A), it's your turn first. Here are your photographs. They show people working together in different situations.

Indicate pictures 3A and 3B on page C7 to Candidate A.

I'd like you to compare the photographs, and say why you think the people are working together in these situations.

All right?

Candidate A: [*1 minute*]

Interlocutor: Thank you.

(Candidate B), do you often work together with your friends? (Why?)

Candidate B: [*Approximately 30 seconds*]

Interlocutor: Thank you.

Now, *(Candidate B)*, here are your photographs. They show people learning to do new things in different situations.

Indicate pictures 3C and 3D on page C8 to Candidate B.

I'd like you to compare the photographs, and say what you think is difficult for the people about learning these things.

All right?

Candidate B: [*1 minute*]

Interlocutor: Thank you.

(Candidate A), which of these things would you like to learn to do? (Why?)

Candidate A: [*Approximately 30 seconds*]

Interlocutor: Thank you.

Parts 3 and 4

Traditions and customs

Part 3 4 minutes (5 minutes for groups of three)

Interlocutor: Now, I'd like you to talk about something together for about two minutes. [*3 minutes for groups of three*]

Some teachers think it's important for students to learn about their country's traditions and customs when they're at school. Here are some of the things they think about and a question for you to discuss. First you have some time to look at the task.

Indicate the visual 3E on page C9 to the candidates. Allow 15 seconds.

Now, talk to each other about whether it's important for students to learn about their country's traditions and customs when they're at school.

Candidates: [*2 minutes / 3 minutes for groups of three*]

Interlocutor: Thank you. Now you have about a minute to decide what you think is the best reason for students to learn about their country's traditions and customs.

Candidates: [*1 minute*]

Interlocutor: Thank you.

Part 4 4 minutes (6 minutes for groups of three)

Interlocutor: *Use the following questions, in order, as appropriate:*

- Is there a custom or tradition in your country that's very popular? (Why do you think it's popular?)
- Do you think it's important to celebrate traditional festivals? (Why? / Why not?)
- Do you think it's true that traditions aren't so important now because countries are becoming more similar? (Why? / Why not?)
- Do you think it is a good idea for schools to organise trips to historic places? (Why? / Why not?)
- Some people say that the best way for children to learn about history is by talking to their grandparents or older people. What do you think?
- Some people say it's more important to study international history and not the history of your own country. Do you agree? (Why? / Why not?)

Select any of the following prompts, as appropriate:

- What do you think?
- Do you agree?
- And you?

Thank you. That is the end of the test.

Test 4

Note: In the examination, there will be both an assessor and an interlocutor in the room.
The visual material for **Test 4** appears on pages C10 and C11 (Part 2), and C12 (Part 3).

Part 1 2 minutes (3 minutes for groups of three)

Interlocutor: Good morning/afternoon/evening. My name is ………… and this is my colleague ………… .
And your names are?
Can I have your mark sheets, please? Thank you.

- Where are you from, *(Candidate A)*?
- And you, *(*Candidate B*)*?

First, we'd like to know something about you.

Select one or more questions from any of the following categories, as appropriate.

Habits and routines
- Do you like to be busy every day? (Why? / Why not?)
- What sport do you enjoy playing? (Why do you like doing that?)
- Do you enjoy watching TV? (What's your favourite programme?) (Why do you like it?)
- Do you ever meet your friends in the evenings after school? (What do you do together?)

The weekend
- Do you prefer to spend time with your family or with your friends at the weekend? (Why?)
- Are there a lot of interesting things to do in your town at the weekend? (What do you do there?)
- Do you often have to do homework at the weekend? (How do you feel about that?)
- Can you tell us something about what you're planning to do next weekend?

The future
- What are you going to do after school today? (Why?)
- What would you like to do for your next birthday? (Why?)
- Is there something you'd like to learn in the future? (What would you like to learn?) (Why?)
- What would you like to do when you leave school? (Why?)

Part 2 4 minutes (6 minutes for groups of three)

Studying science
Spending time alone

Interlocutor: In this part of the test, I'm going to give each of you two photographs. I'd like you to talk about your photographs on your own for about a minute, and also to answer a question about your partner's photographs.

(Candidate A), it's your turn first. Here are your photographs. They show people studying science in different ways.

Indicate pictures 4A and 4B on page C10 to Candidate A.

I'd like you to compare the photographs, and say what you think the advantages are of studying science in these ways.

All right?

Candidate A: [*1 minute*]

Interlocutor: Thank you.

(Candidate B), do you enjoy studying science? (Why?)

Candidate B: [*Approximately 30 seconds*]

Interlocutor: Thank you.

Now, *(Candidate B)*, here are your photographs. They show people spending time on their own.

Indicate pictures 4C and 4D on page C11 to Candidate B.

I'd like you to compare the photographs, and say why you think these people have decided to spend time on their own.

All right?

Candidate B: [*1 minute*]

Interlocutor: Thank you.

(Candidate A), do you like spending time on your own? (Why?)

Candidate A: [*Approximately 30 seconds*]

Interlocutor: Thank you.

Parts 3 and 4

Spending time outdoors

Part 3 4 minutes (5 minutes for groups of three)

Interlocutor: Now, I'd like you to talk about something together for about two minutes. [*3 minutes for groups of three*]

Some people think teenagers should spend most of their free time outdoors with their friends. Here are some things they think about and a question for you to discuss. First you have some time to look at the task.

Indicate the visual 4E on page C12 to the candidates. Allow 15 seconds.

Now, talk to each other about whether teenagers should spend most of their free time outdoors with their friends.

Candidates: [*2 minutes / 3 minutes for groups of three*]

Interlocutor: Thank you. Now you have about a minute to decide what you think is the most important reason for teenagers to spend their free time outdoors with their friends.

Candidates: [*1 minute*]

Interlocutor: Thank you.

Part 4 4 minutes (6 minutes for groups of three)

Interlocutor: *Use the following questions, in order, as appropriate:*

- Do you and your friends spend a lot of your time doing outdoor activities? (Why? / Why not?)
- Should students have to do outdoor sports lessons at school? (Why? / Why not?)
- Do you think it's a good idea for families to go on holidays where they spend a lot of time outside, for example camping holidays? (Why? / Why not?)
- Is growing up in the countryside better for children than living in cities? (Why? / Why not?)
- Some people say that it is important for big cities to have good parks. Do you agree? (Why? / Why not?)
- Do you think it's true that if people spent more time outside, they'd care more about protecting the environment? (Why? / Why not?)

Select any of the following prompts, as appropriate:

- What do you think?
- Do you agree?
- And you?

Thank you. That is the end of the test.

Marks and results

Reading and Use of English

Candidates record their answers on a separate answer sheet. One mark is given for each correct answer in Parts 1, 2, 3 and 7. For Part 4, candidates are awarded a mark of 2, 1 or 0 for each question according to the accuracy of their response. Correct spelling is required in Parts 2, 3 and 4. Two marks are given for each correct answer in Parts 5 and 6.

Candidates will receive separate scores for Reading and for Use of English. The total marks candidates achieve for each section are converted into a score on the Cambridge English Scale. These are equally weighted when calculating the overall score on the scale (an average of the individual scores for the four skills and Use of English).

Writing

Examiners look at four aspects of your writing: Content, Communicative Achievement, Organisation and Language.

- Content focuses on how well you have fulfilled the task, in other words if you have done what you were asked to do.
- Communicative Achievement focuses on how appropriate the writing is for the task and whether you have used the appropriate register.
- Organisation focuses on the way you put the piece of writing together, in other words if it is logical and ordered.
- Language focuses on your vocabulary and grammar. This includes the range of language as well as how accurate it is.

For each of the subscales, the examiner gives a maximum of 5 marks. Examiners use the following assessment scale:

B2	Content	Communicative Achievement	Organisation	Language
5	All content is relevant to the task. Target reader is fully informed.	Uses the conventions of the communicative task effectively to hold the target reader's attention and communicate straightforward and complex ideas, as appropriate.	Text is well organised and coherent, using a variety of cohesive devices and organisational patterns to generally good effect.	Uses a range of vocabulary, including less common lexis, appropriately. Uses a range of simple and complex grammatical forms with control and flexibility. Occasional errors may be present but do not impede communication.
4	*Performance shares features of Bands 3 and 5.*			

3	Minor irrelevances and/ or omissions may be present. Target reader is on the whole informed.	Uses the conventions of the communicative task to hold the target reader's attention and communicate straightforward ideas.	Text is generally well organised and coherent, using a variety of linking words and cohesive devices.	Uses a range of everyday vocabulary appropriately, with occasional inappropriate use of less common lexis. Uses a range of simple and some complex grammatical forms with a good degree of control. Errors do not impede communication.
2	*Performance shares features of Bands 1 and 3.*			
1	Irrelevances and misinterpretation of task may be present. Target reader is minimally informed.	Uses the conventions of the communicative task in generally appropriate ways to communicate straightforward ideas.	Text is connected and coherent, using basic linking words and a limited number of cohesive devices.	Uses everyday vocabulary generally appropriately, while occasionally overusing certain lexis. Uses simple grammatical forms with a good degree of control. While errors are noticeable, meaning can still be determined.
0	Content is totally irrelevant. Target reader is not informed.	*Performance below Band 1.*		

Length of responses

Make sure you write the correct number of words. Responses which are too short may not have an adequate range of language and may not provide all the information that is required. Responses which are too long may contain irrelevant content and have a negative effect on the reader.

Varieties of English

You are expected to use a particular variety of English with some degree of consistency in areas such as spelling, and not for example switch from using a British spelling of a word to an American spelling of the same word.

Writing sample answers and examiner's comments

The following pieces of writing have been selected from students' answers. The samples relate to tasks in Tests 1–4. Explanatory notes have been added to show how the marks have been arrived at.

Sample A (Test 1, Question 1 – Essay)

> *Is it better for teenagers to make their own decisions or to ask for advice from other people?*
>
> *In my opinion teenagers can make their own decisions regarding some aspects of their lives, while they definitely need counselling for others.*
>
> *For example, choosing clothes should be done by teenagers, so they develop their own style. Furthermore, this gives them a sense of freedom of expression and they feel they can do what they want*
>
> *On the other hand, there are issues like choosing the subjects to study or the future career where they need the advice of either their parents, or a counsellor or both. I think it may be difficult for a young person to know for sure what career to choose. Moreover, jobs that might seem appealling at first, can be tricky, and it is the experience and expertise of an adult that can help e teenager make the right decision.*
>
> *In conclusion, it is my strong belief that teenagers and adults should talk about important issues such as career and studies, while clothes should be left to teenagers.*

Scales	Mark	Commentary
Content	5	All content is relevant to the task and the target reader is fully informed. The writer refers to the two given points and includes their own idea, choosing a job.
Communicative Achievement	5	The conventions of essay writing are used effectively, with appropriate use of common essay expressions (*In my opinion; Furthermore; In conclusion*) to structure the argument. The writer presents a balanced argument, supporting each point with an explanation and concluding with a clear statement of their opinion on the topic. Ideas, including some more complex ones (*Moreover, jobs that … right decision*), are communicated clearly and the target reader's attention is held throughout.
Organisation	5	The text is well-organised and coherent. Each paragraph addresses a separate point in the discussion and ideas are connected within and across sentences and paragraphs by effective use of a range of cohesive devices and organisational patterns, including referencing, substitution and ellipsis.
Language	5	A range of vocabulary including some less common lexis (*counselling; freedom of expression; appealling; expertise*), is used appropriately. There is a range of simple and more complex grammatical forms, including passive and modal structures and relative clauses, used with control and flexibility. Errors are minimal and do not impede communication.

Sample B (Test 1, Question 3 – Email)

> *Dear Naomi,*
>
> *Hi friend! I hope you and your family are okey. I received your email yesterday but I was too busy to replayed you.*
>
> *You don't have to be worried, I admite it can be hard at the start but then you'll be okey with that. I remembered when Emily, my friend who moved recently, told the same things that you're telling me now, but now Emi is really happy and have some friends.*
>
> *I can advise you about one thing: Don't be shy and try to be more sociable. I know you too much and I have to tell you that you need to be more self-confident and you have to show like you really are. Don't be scared of meeting new people and make friends.*
>
> *About living on a new place it's not a problem or a thing to be worried. We're again on the same point, you have to be sociable and then you're goind to adapt to the city. You can walking in the city with your family to know more about it and how the population act or what they do.*
>
> *Sorry but I must go because my mum is calling me. I hope you'll be okey. Keep in touch.*
>
> *Loves you,*
>
> *Nora*

Scales	Mark	Commentary
Content	5	All content is relevant to the task and the target reader is fully informed on all points in the question.
Communicative Achievement	3	The conventions of an informal email are used generally appropriately (*Dear Naomi; Hi friend! I hope ... okey; Sorry but I must go; Keep in touch; Loves you*). The writer addresses the target reader directly and gives reassurance, suitable advice and suggestions based on personal experience, all of which engages and holds the reader's attention
Organisation	3	The text is generally well-organised and coherent. Topic sentences are used to signal the focus of each paragraph and ideas are connected using a reasonable variety of linking words and cohesive devices, such as referencing pronouns. A greater range of cohesive devices to connect ideas in longer sentences would improve the overall cohesiveness of the text.
Language	3	A range of everyday vocabulary (*sociable; self-confident; adapt*) is used appropriately, despite some spelling errors. There is a range of grammatical forms used with a good degree of control. Errors, for example with prepositions and subject/verb agreement, do not impede communication.

Sample C (Test 2, Question 1 – Essay)

Now a days, it is too dificult for parents to have control about their children at home. There have to be some rules for living together.

In one point of view, having rules at home is very important, because children do what they want with out those. For example, the have to help with jobs around the house. They have to order their bathroom and their bedroom, do the washing up and clear the floor when their mom needs help. Also, they should have a good actitude at meal-times. For example, eat all their food and do not use their mobile phone. The last one is a really bad habit that they have to change.

Another point of view, is about parents who don't care about they children do. Because of this, their children do what they want, don't help at home, don't sit down in meal-times and they use their phone every time. Parents thinks that don't be extrict with their children is correct and good for they.

In conclusion, is a good idea have rules at home and control ower children for create good habits for their life.

Scales	Mark	Commentary
Content	4	The content is relevant to the task. The target reader is informed about the two given points: jobs around the house and behaviour at meal times. Rather than introducing and developing a separate 'own idea', the third paragraph presents a contrasting situation for these points. There is a brief reference to the parents' attitude, but this is not developed as a separate point and so the target reader is not fully informed.
Communicative Achievement	3	The conventions of essay writing, with generally suitable expressions for the genre (*In one point of view; Another point of view; For example; In conclusion*), are used appropriately to communicate straightforward ideas. The writer presents a balanced argument which leads to a clear conclusion and the target reader's attention is held.
Organisation	3	The text is generally well-organised and coherent. Paragraphing, linking words and some cohesive devices (*because children do what they want with out those; The last one; Because of this*) are used generally appropriately to connect ideas at sentence and paragraph level.
Language	3	A range of everyday vocabulary is used appropriately, despite some problems with spelling. There is a range of simple grammatical forms used with a good degree of control. The errors, mainly with pronouns, do not impede communication.

Sample D (Test 2, Question 4 – Story)

> *Mark was walking along the beach one Saturday morning. He loved to wake up early, and then relax there, by the sea, watching the birds and the boats sailing far away.*
>
> *He was thinking about the exciting school trip he had had last week when, suddently, he heard an awful noise. What on earth could that be? He was a bit worried, but as he didn't hear that strenge sound again, he started to relax. But he heard it again, it was louder. This time, Mark recognised the sound: it was a girl's scream.*
>
> *Mark looked around for the place where the sound came from, and he found it. A girl was drowning, and he didn't think it twice: he started to swim to get to her as soon as possible. After a minute or two, he was very tired, but he kept swimming, - Don't worry! I'll save you! – said Mark*
>
> *And at last, he did it. Mark saved the girl, and they both returned without any injury.*
>
> *- You have saved my life, thanks! – said the blond hair girl to Mark.*
>
> *And they became the best friends ever.*

Scales	Mark	Commentary
Content	5	All content is relevant to the task. The story follows logically from the prompt sentence and includes the two given points: *he heard an awful noise; Mark saved the girl.*
Communicative Achievement	4	The conventions of story writing, with a clear narrative development, rhetorical questions, direct speech and a suitable ending, are used effectively to engage and hold the reader's interest. The first paragraph sets the scene and the situation for the action is established at the start of the second paragraph. A combination of short and long sentences moves the action forward and creates suspense, motivating the reader to keep going to find out what happens.
Organisation	5	The text is well-organised and coherent, with effective use of organisational patterns to reflect the storyline and rhetorical questions and direct speech to move the action forward. Moving from short to longer paragraphs and sentences and back again mirrors the suspense of the action. Referencing and a range of cohesive devices are used effectively to connect ideas at sentence and paragraph level.
Language	4	A range of vocabulary is used generally effectively (*What on earth; drowning; he didn't think it twice; without any injury*), with just a few spelling errors. There is a range of simple and complex grammatical forms, including a range of narrative tenses, used with control and flexibility. Errors are minimal and do not impede communication.

Sample E (Test 3, Question 1 – Essay)

Nowadays, we notice more doors opening for young people providing them with many appealing opportunities, which we certainly cannot say was happening in the past and I am going to prove that.

To begin with, these days there definitely is more universities, which also offer many different courses than in the past. Furthermore there is no longer any reason why girls would not be able to expand their knowledge.

Morover, in the past people were only able to read books or go outside, whereas in present there is no issue with finding something interesting to do, for example a playing computer games or watching movies online.

Lastly, in the past people were expected to start a family at a rather young age. What comes with that, women had to stay at home and take care of children, while men were supposed to work to be able to financialy support an entire family. People were also dying at a younger age.

In conclusion, I think we can surely say that in the present we are given more oportunities to develop our personalities and reach our goals than young people were in the past and I am really grateful for that.

Scales	Mark	Commentary
Content	4	The content is relevant to the task. The writer presents a well-developed response to the question and discusses education and two of their own ideas, the impact of technology on leisure and the role of women in society. There is no reference to one of the given points, travel, and so the target reader is not fully informed.
Communicative Achievement	5	The conventions of essay writing are used effectively to hold the target reader's attention and communicate straightforward and complex ideas, for example when contrasting opportunities for men and for women. The opening paragraph presents a clear statement of the writer's opinion which is then explored through a balanced argument that uses examples and explanations and leads to a strong conclusion and personal response.
Organisation	4	The text is well-organised and coherent. The development of the argument is supported by effective paragraphing and a range of cohesive devices is used effectively to signal and develop each new point and connect ideas both within and across sentences and paragraphs.
Language	4	There is a range of vocabulary used effectively (*more doors opening; appealing opportunities; expand their knowledge*), with a few spelling errors. A range of simple and some more complex grammatical forms, including passive forms and modals, is used with control and flexibility. The errors which are present do not impede communication.

Sample F (Test 3, Question 4 – Review)

> *One of the best games and toy shops is the one on Flower Street, 357: „Miss Margaret Toy Shop". It has very cute decorations outside the shop, but inside too. The employers are very nice and helps you if you if you don't know what you're looking for. The aisles are separated on kids ages and there aren't too violent games or + 18. There are toys and games for almost every age and you can find anything very easily because they are very organised. The shop is actualised with the newest toys and games every month and unlike other shops, the prices are cheaper on most of them. There are expensive ones too, but the price is worth it, to be honest.*
>
> *It is in a hidden place so that's why it's not so visited, but I think it's a great toy shop and this review would help them get the customers and appreciation they deserve.*

Scales	Mark	Commentary
Content	5	All content is relevant to the task and the target reader is fully informed about the shop, what it sells and why the writer thinks it's a good place to buy toys and games.
Communicative Achievement	3	The conventions of review writing are used to communicate straightforward ideas. There is an appropriate balance of factual information and personal comments to inform and hold the reader's attention and the final comment is effective in encouraging the reader to visit the shop.
Organisation	3	The text is generally well-organised and coherent. A variety of linking words and cohesive devices (*It has; because they are; There are expensive ones too; that's why*) are used to connect ideas. Paragraphing to signal key points in the review and a greater range of cohesive devices to connect ideas between sentences and paragraphs would improve the overall cohesiveness of the text.
Language	3	There is a range of everyday vocabulary used appropriately (*cute decorations; hidden place; get the customers and appreciation they deserve*), with occasional inappropriate use of less common lexis (*actualised*). There is a range of simple grammatical forms used with a good degree of control. Minor errors with, for example, prepositions and comparative forms, do not impede communication.

Sample G (Test 4, Question 1 – Essay)

> *There are some people who say that the schools will change in the future.*
>
> *1. The teachers will change a lot. In the future, all the teachers will be robots, which is not a good thing, because robots do not have any feelings, it are machines. This will be like that because robots are faster in almost everything.*
>
> *2. Another difference will be that the subjects will be different. The students in the future will have more math, but less languages. This will be like that, because when they are good at math they can understand the robot-teachers better.*
>
> *3. Another thing will be the fact that the children will not have to come to a school building, but they can stay at home and follow the lessons from there. This will need a new software, which is controlled by robots, who are also the teachers.*
>
> *So, the schools will change a lot, but the things that are going to change, are, in my opinion, not good things, because it all will not be controlled by humans and I will keep a world, which is controlled by humanity.*

Scales	Mark	Commentary
Content	5	All content is relevant to the task and the target reader is informed about the two given points and the writer's own idea, studying from home.
Communicative Achievement	3	The conventions of essay writing are followed to communicate straightforward ideas. There is a simple introduction and, despite the unusual approach of numbering the individual points, the communicative purpose of giving opinions on the topic is achieved and the target reader's attention is held. The concluding paragraph effectively summarises the points made and communicates the writer's opinion on the topic.
Organisation	3	The text is generally well-organised and coherent. There is evidence of a range of cohesive devices used with flexibility in the final paragraph, but, overall, simple linking is used to introduce the focus of each paragraph and connect ideas within and across sentences. A greater variety of cohesive devices to connect ideas in longer sentences and across paragraphs would improve the overall cohesiveness of the text.
Language	4	A range of everyday vocabulary is used appropriately and there is a range of generally simple grammatical forms used with control. A greater range of future and conditional forms would be appropriate for this communicative task. Occasional errors do not impede communication.

Sample H (Test 4, Question 2 – Article)

> *Weather. We can all hear or read the magical predictions of it on the radio, television or the internet. It may look like this topic is of vital importance to all of us, yet I personally am of different opinion. My view on this matter might seem cynical, as I don't care much about the weather, but I can still say a word about the effects different kinds of weather have on us.*
>
> *To start with, I think I can safely say that the bright, optimist, sunshiny day is the epitome of a happy mood. although I am no exception to this, I think I may be one in my attitude to a dark, rainy weather, which certainly is one of the things which turns anyone's day into a bad one. Surprisingly, I sometimes fancy this "black sheep" of the weather family and I seem to enjoy the walks with my dog a lot more.*
>
> *That's it to my article about weather. I wish only the most awesome weather to all of you!*

Scales	Mark	Commentary
Content	5	All content is relevant to the task and the target reader is fully informed about the writer's attitudes to the weather and the effect it has on their mood.
Communicative Achievement	5	The article is written in an engaging style which is appropriate. The one word opening sentence is an effective way of attracting the reader's attention and introducing the topic, which is then explored using a natural, informal tone, before concluding with a strong final sentence which addresses the reader directly. Straightforward and more complex ideas, for example in the second paragraph, are communicated effectively.
Organisation	5	The text is well-organised and coherent. Internal and external cohesion is established through a variety of cohesive devices and organisational patterns used with flexibility, moving from general to personal statements and paraphrasing appropriately to avoid repetition (*Weather … this matter … one of the things … this "black sheep" of the weather family*).
Language	5	There is a range of vocabulary, including less common lexis (*cynical; I can safely say; epitome; black sheep*), used appropriately and naturally. A range of simple and complex grammatical forms is used with control and flexibility, creating a natural flow to the article. Errors are minimal and communication is not impeded.

Listening

One mark is given for each correct answer. The total mark is converted into a score on the Cambridge English Scale for the paper. In Part 2, minor spelling errors are allowed, provided that the candidate's intention is clear.

For security reasons, several versions of the Listening paper are used at each administration of the examination. Before grading, the performance of the candidates in each of the versions is compared and marks adjusted to compensate for any imbalance in levels of difficulty.

Speaking

Throughout the test candidates are assessed on their own individual performance and not in relation to the other candidate. They are assessed on their language skills, not on their personality, intelligence or knowledge of the world. Candidates must, however, be prepared to develop the conversation and respond to the tasks in an appropriate way.

Candidates are awarded marks by two examiners: the assessor and the interlocutor. The assessor awards marks by applying performance descriptors from the Analytical Assessment scales for the following criteria:

Grammar and Vocabulary

This refers to the accurate use of grammatical forms and appropriate use of vocabulary. It also includes the range of language.

Discourse Management

This refers to the extent, relevance and coherence of each candidate's contributions. Candidates should be able to construct clear stretches of speech which are easy to follow. The length of their contributions should be appropriate to the task, and what they say should be related to the topic and the conversation in general.

Pronunciation

This refers to the intelligibility of contributions at word and sentence levels. Candidates should be able to produce utterances that can easily be understood, and which show control of intonation, stress and individual sounds.

Interactive Communication

This refers to the ability to use language to achieve meaningful communication. Candidates should be able to initiate and respond appropriately according to the task and conversation, and also to use interactive strategies to maintain and develop the communication whilst negotiating towards an outcome.

B2	Grammar and Vocabulary	Discourse Management	Pronunciation	Interactive Communication
5	• Shows a good degree of control of a range of simple and some complex grammatical forms. • Uses a range of appropriate vocabulary to give and exchange views on a wide range of familiar topics.	• Produces extended stretches of language with very little hesitation. • Contributions are relevant and there is a clear organisation of ideas. • Uses a range of cohesive devices and discourse markers.	• Is intelligible. • Intonation is appropriate. • Sentence and word stress is accurately placed. • Individual sounds are articulated clearly.	• Initiates and responds appropriately, linking contributions to those of other speakers. • Maintains and develops the interaction and negotiates towards an outcome.
4	*Performance shares features of Bands 3 and 5.*			
3	• Shows a good degree of control of simple grammatical forms, and attempts some complex grammatical forms. • Uses a range of appropriate vocabulary to give and exchange views on a range of familiar topics.	• Produces extended stretches of language despite some hesitation. • Contributions are relevant and there is very little repetition. • Uses a range of cohesive devices.	• Is intelligible. • Intonation is generally appropriate. • Sentence and word stress is generally accurately placed. • Individual sounds are generally articulated clearly.	• Initiates and responds appropriately. • Maintains and develops the interaction and negotiates towards an outcome with very little support.
2	*Performance shares features of Bands 1 and 3.*			
1	• Shows a good degree of control of simple grammatical forms. • Uses a range of appropriate vocabulary when talking about everyday situations.	• Produces responses which are extended beyond short phrases, despite hesitation. • Contributions are mostly relevant, despite some repetition. • Uses basic cohesive devices.	• Is mostly intelligible, and has some control of phonological features at both utterance and word levels.	• Initiates and responds appropriately. • Keeps the interaction going with very little prompting and support.
0	*Performance below Band 1.*			

The interlocutor awards a mark for overall performance using a Global Achievement scale.

B2	Global Achievement
5	• Handles communication on a range of familiar topics, with very little hesitation. • Uses accurate and appropriate linguistic resources to express ideas and produce extended discourse that is generally coherent.
4	*Performance shares features of Bands 3 and 5.*
3	• Handles communication on familiar topics, despite some hesitation. • Organises extended discourse but occasionally produces utterances that lack coherence, and some inaccuracies and inappropriate usage occur.
2	*Performance shares features of Bands 1 and 3.*
1	• Handles communication in everyday situations, despite hesitation. • Constructs longer utterances but is not able to use complex language except in well-rehearsed utterances.
0	*Performance below Band 1.*

Assessment for *Cambridge English: First for Schools* is based on performance across all parts of the test, and is achieved by applying the relevant descriptors in the assessment scales.

Test 1 Key

Reading and Use of English (1 hour 15 minutes)

Part 1

1 C **2** B **3** D **4** A **5** D **6** C **7** D **8** B

Part 2

9 If **10** out **11** What **12** made **13** of **14** is **15** who/that **16** up

Part 3

17 impressive **18** popularity **19** relief **20** inexperienced
21 hopeless **22** surroundings **23** memorable **24** passionate

Part 4

25 hadn't / had not EXPECTED | to see
26 PUT us | up
27 cannot/can't | be BOTHERED
28 keep | an EYE on
29 to DISCOURAGE Jo/her | from eating/having
30 to take | ACCOUNT of/into ACCOUNT

Part 5

31 B **32** B **33** A **34** D **35** C **36** C

Part 6

37 E **38** C **39** A **40** F **41** D **42** G

Part 7

43 C **44** A **45** E **46** D **47** B **48** C **49** A **50** B **51** D **52** E

Writing (1 hour 20 minutes)

Candidate responses are marked using the assessment scale on page 107-108.

Listening (approximately 40 minutes)

Part 1

1 C **2** A **3** A **4** C **5** C **6** A **7** B **8** B

Part 2

9 magazine **10** harbour **11** sunrise **12** magical **13** size
14 30/thirty **15** population(s) **16** baby **17** Zebra **18** India

Part 3

19 C **20** D **21** H **22** B **23** F

Part 4

24 B **25** B **26** A **27** C **28** C **29** B **30** A

Transcript

This is the Cambridge English: First for Schools Listening Test. Test One.

I'm going to give you the instructions for this test. I'll introduce each part of the test and give you time to look at the questions. At the start of each piece you'll hear this sound:

tone

You will hear each piece twice.

Remember, while you're listening, write your answers on the question paper. You'll have five minutes at the end of the test to copy your answers onto the separate answer sheet.

There will now be a pause. Please ask any questions now, because you must not speak during the test.

[pause]

Now open your question paper and look at Part One.

[pause]

PART 1

You'll hear people talking in eight different situations. For questions 1 to 8, choose the best answer (A, B or C).

Question 1 — *You hear a singer talking about performing on stage.*

[pause]

tone

Woman: I'm quite nervous before a performance. Experts say the way to handle that is to imagine you're singing to an empty room rather than a theatre full of people. I tried that – it's easier said than done though. But I saw another singer I worked with doing deep breathing exercises before going on stage. She encouraged me to have a go and, although it probably worked better for her than for me, it is quite effective. I didn't use to chat much with anyone before going on stage 'cos I was worried it might affect my concentration, but these days I need to discuss last-minute stuff with the band and technical guys.

[pause]

tone

[The recording is repeated.]

[pause]

Question 2 — *You hear a girl telling her father about a special day at school.*

[pause]

tone

Girl: We had to go to school dressed as a character from a novel today, for World Book Day. I went dressed as a character from one of my favourite books.

Man: You worked hard on that costume.

Girl: Yeah, my sewing skills are hopeless, but everyone said I looked fantastic.

Man: Good. Were there any special activities organized?

Girl: Someone called Linda Martin who writes novels for teenagers gave a talk. Apparently she's famous.

Man: Really?

Girl: And then I was interviewed by two girls from another class who wanted to know what I thought about the day in general. They were doing a class magazine. I'm not sure why they chose me, but it was fun anyway.

Man: Great!

[pause]

tone

[The recording is repeated.]

[pause]

Question 3 *You hear two friends talking about a summer camp they could both go on.*

[pause]

tone

Girl: You know that summer camp we were told about, where you learn how to design video games and apps? Would you fancy going on it?

Boy: I like the idea of learning how to write computer code. Whether I could manage two whole weeks doing the same stuff is another thing.

Girl: You've got a point. There'd be other stuff to do, though – like sports and trips.

Boy: Maybe. But once we were there, we'd be stuck and we wouldn't even have our own rooms. And I've never spent that long without my family before.

Girl: It would take some getting used to. There'd be other people our age, though.

Boy: There's no knowing we'd like them.

[pause]

tone

[The recording is repeated.]

[pause]

Question 4 *You hear a boy talking about his favourite TV programme.*

[pause]

tone

Boy: I love *Princes of the North*! I study history at school so I really appreciate the way the writers mention actual kings and queens. The plots are very clever with all the twists and turns. But this does mean that the main people in the story suddenly do unexpected things that don't seem to be consistent with what they did in earlier episodes, and you're just trying to figure out why. The current series has been criticised because there's a feeling that they've cut out all the fantasy, which was such a big feature of the first series. There's still plenty of excitement though if that's what you're looking for.

[pause]

tone

[The recording is repeated.]

[pause]

Question 5 *You hear a journalist talking about an unusual type of house.*

[pause]

tone

Man: This winter's been particularly harsh for people living in Boston in the USA. One enterprising resident's had the idea of building himself an igloo. It's not unlike an Eskimo igloo in design, so it's quite unusual to see it standing in the city. The owner's currently offering short igloo breaks at an affordable ten dollars a night and there's been a lot of interest. It seems people can't wait to spend a night in the freezing cold and I'm actually one of them – although I know it's not for everyone. And although the owner's hoping it might take off in other areas of the country, this doesn't seem too likely to me.

[pause]

tone

[The recording is repeated.]

[pause]

Question 6 *You hear part of an interview with a boy called Max, who found a prehistoric object.*

[pause]

tone

Woman: People often dream of discovering ancient objects, but fourteen-year-old Max Simmons has actually done it. Tell us about your discovery, Max.

Boy: There's a beach where I go to look for old stuff. Recently I found a stone which looked like an arrowhead. My dad reckoned it wasn't, but I took it to a museum and they said it is an arrowhead and it's over fourteen thousand years old.

Woman: Good thing you didn't listen to your dad!

Boy: Yeah. I'm trusting my own judgment from now on.

Woman: Were your friends impressed?

Boy: Well, they asked me all about it but they think searching for prehistoric stuff's weird. I think it's brilliant to find something someone used so long ago.

[pause]

tone

[The recording is repeated.]

[pause]

Question 7 *You hear a girl talking about the sport called netball.*

[pause]

tone

Girl: I've always thought netball's a really great sport and I've enjoyed playing it, but I just can't believe how much time some girls at my school spend practising in the gym so that they're fit enough to get picked for the big matches. I've always managed to get into the team without doing that. There's more than one version of the game and the rules vary depending on which version you play. The best ways to move around the court, and how to throw and catch the ball effectively aren't things you can pick up just like that in a few training sessions – so learning how to play well is challenging, but it's fun.

[pause]

tone

[The recording is repeated.]

[pause]

Question 8 *You hear two friends discussing a news story about some rock climbers.*

[pause]

tone

Girl: Did you see those two climbers on the news? They were the first people to climb that 800-metre cliff. It was a vertical rock-face. Terrifying!

Boy: And they did it without any equipment – apart from safety ropes!

Girl: Yes – they even had to sleep in tents hanging from the cliff during the climb. I can't imagine doing that!

Boy: I'd love to do something like that. It makes me want to join a climbing club – I don't think I'd be brave enough though. And I wonder how their families felt about them doing it.

Girl: They must have been really worried, don't you think?

Boy: I imagine they'd have been proud more than anything.

[pause]

tone

[The recording is repeated.]

[pause]

That's the end of Part One.

Now turn to Part Two.

[pause]

PART 2

You'll hear a woman called Ingrid talking about doing volunteer work on a shark conservation project on the island of Fiji. For questions 9 to 18, complete the sentences with a word or short phrase.

You now have forty-five seconds to look at Part Two.

[pause]

tone

Ingrid: Last summer, before starting university, I spent two months volunteering on the island of Fiji in the South Pacific Ocean for a research programme called Project Shark. You may well fancy doing something similar when you finish school. There's an excellent website telling you about it if you want to find out more – I looked through that after I'd read an article about the programme in a magazine. It also has links to a blog, where I discovered more about the project from previous volunteers.

What initially appealed to me was the chance to go diving. I grew up on the coast and my dad used to dive in a harbour not far from where we lived. When I was about fifteen, I went with him and he showed me the basics. The local swimming pool had diving lessons too, which I'm sure would've been good – I didn't need to spend the money on them, though.

The journey to Fiji took about 35 hours. I was so exhausted when I got there that I don't remember much about my first day. I took the bus from the airport to the project and must've passed through some beautiful scenery to get there, I suppose, but I slept through all that. I did see the sunrise though – that'll stay with me forever.

The aim of Project Shark is to gather information about sharks and use it to work out how to protect them from environmental threats. Diving in places where sharks live can give you good data. I know it sounds frightening, but you just have to know what you're doing and volunteers are always accompanied by experts. It's magical, though, when you've got sharks swimming all around you.

One type of shark they're studying is called the Bull Shark. The upper bodies of these sharks are a strange grey colour, and their noses are broad and flat. What struck me about these sharks was their size, actually. You wouldn't want to fight with one. And usually, when I think of sharks hunting for food, I think of the speed they go at, but Bull Sharks are relatively slow. Bull Sharks like shallow waters near the coast, so generally we didn't dive deeper than about 5 metres. Sometimes, though, we went further out to where it was 30 metres down to the seabed – that was satisfying because it was much further down than my previous record of twenty-two metres. When you're down there, your eyes adjust to the darkness and the three-and-a-half metre Bull Sharks appear around you – amazing!

Divers investigate a range of things. It's important to study different shark habitats. How big the populations of different shark species are is another thing they get data on, and that's what I was mostly involved in. They also did a survey of shark behaviour, which I found fascinating.

One thing researchers do is insert a metal tag containing a tiny transmitter under a shark's skin – they can then follow the shark's movements. Bull Sharks are tracked like this, but scientists target the baby animals 'cos they're easier to handle than the adult Bull Sharks. I learnt a lot doing that.

I got to see other types of sharks, not just Bull Sharks. A Tiger Shark once got really close to me, and the Hammerhead Sharks are relatively easy to spot because they're quite common. There was no sign of any Zebra Sharks when I went there, which was a pity, 'cos they're supposed to look amazing. I also missed out on seeing Great White Sharks – but they're not the friendliest species so I wasn't too bothered about that!

Apart from the diving and research, I loved being with the other volunteers who came from all over the world. I shared a room with a nice girl from Japan, and on the dives, I was often paired with a girl from India – we got along really well and we still talk on social media. There was also a guy from Australia who gave me surfing lessons and we emailed for a while when I first got back.

Well, I'll stop talking now – have you …

[pause]

Now you'll hear Part Two again.

tone

[The recording is repeated.]

[pause]

That's the end of Part Two.

Now turn to Part Three.

[pause]

PART 3

You'll hear five short extracts in which teenagers are talking about their experience of doing experiments in science lessons at school. For questions 19 to 23, choose from the list (A to H) how each speaker feels about their experience. Use the letters only once. There are three extra letters which you do not need to use.

You now have thirty seconds to look at Part Three.

[pause]

tone

Speaker 1

Boy: When we're doing experiments in class, our science teacher normally explains everything to us in great detail, but I remember one science lesson when she decided to let us work things out for ourselves. Some of my friends weren't happy, but I thought this was a cool idea. After discussing it in groups, everyone knew what they were doing and had a clear role. It was a pity we were working under time pressure though. I reckon that must've affected the quality of the work because the results were all over the place. It would've been better to repeat the whole thing at least once more.

[pause]

Speaker 2

Girl: I used to struggle with science, so I was often fed up and blamed my teacher for the way I felt. Then one day we had to do an experiment and everything that could go wrong, did go wrong. I noticed I wasn't the only one having problems so that stopped me feeling too bad. But the teacher told us that all the slips and all the miscalculations didn't matter because you learn from them, and they're part of doing science. That made me feel more positive and like I can really achieve something in science now.

[pause]

Speaker 3

Boy: I did this interesting science experiment in class the other day. We had to do everything in about forty-five minutes – we got a bit worked up at first because we thought there'd be problems, especially as we had to repeat the experiment a few times. In the end, having a strict deadline actually helped us get things done, and repeating things wasn't a big deal – we just got better at all the techniques. My friend had the job of presenting the results, but he made a complete mess of it. I guess he didn't have a system. I wasn't too pleased about that because we'd been working well as a group till then.

[pause]

Speaker 4

Girl: I did quite a complicated chemistry experiment the other day – well I found the teacher's explanation slightly confusing, though it sort of made sense later! We were told to do the experiment several times just to make sure our results were reliable. I made a fairly basic mistake almost immediately, of course, but I managed not to get upset about it, so nobody noticed. But it meant I had to change my plan halfway through and use a different piece of equipment. I thought that was quite impressive really because science subjects aren't my thing, and I sometimes panic if things go wrong. But I was pleased that my results turned out OK.

[pause]

Speaker 5

Boy: In my science class, we had to design our own experiment. The whole idea of this was not to go running to the teacher asking for help every five minutes and to do everything against the clock. I liked the challenge of not having much time, but I could see other people were panicking and weren't doing things in a sensible order. I sort of thought I wouldn't get the outcome I hoped for, especially because I couldn't repeat the experiment, which was a pain. But though things weren't perfect, the data I ended up with was pretty accurate. I'd been quite worried, to be honest.

[pause]

Now you'll hear Part Three again.

tone

[The recording is repeated.]

[pause]

That's the end of Part Three.

Now turn to Part Four.

PART 4

You'll hear an interview with an air traffic controller called Jake Watson, whose job involves directing aircraft in and out of an airport. For questions 24 to 30, choose the best answer (A, B or C).

You now have one minute to look at Part Four.

[pause]

tone

Interviewer: With me on *Careers Talk* is Jake Watson, who's an air traffic controller – making sure planes take off and land safely at a busy airport. Jake, welcome! We've got many questions, emailed by our teenage listeners.

Jake: OK!

Interviewer: First, Sarah asks what you find challenging about your job.

Jake: The job's extremely interesting but it's not easy. Obviously it involves keeping radio contact with aircraft and directing their movements. I also have to provide information to pilots about weather conditions, for example. So there's a lot involved. I get to use advanced radio communication to maintain contact with pilots. I also speak to air authorities to make sure planes pass safely through their airspace. And it's when I have to deal with all this at once that I'm really stretched.

Interviewer: Ben asks how you ended up doing such an unusual job!

Jake: I've always loved being around airports! After graduating in aircraft engineering, I got my private pilot's licence – I'd always wanted to become a commercial pilot. But then I was offered a job in aircraft maintenance. That was pressured at times, so it was good training – and I was lucky enough to be getting a good salary. But after a while it became a bit routine, so I started looking at what else was available and saw the job advertised.

Interviewer: Samantha wants to know how hard it was to get the job.

Jake: The selection process was tough. I was given lots of tasks, like problem-solving to test my analytical skills – which I'd been nervous about. To my surprise, I had no problems with them. I've always been good at math, which probably helped. Actually, I thought math would be a basic necessity for this work and that doing the job would make me even better at it. In fact, only straightforward calculations are involved. Anyway, I got through!

Interviewer: Peter asks how you felt when you first took charge of landing a plane without any help.

Jake: Yes, well, as a trainee, you're used to having someone listening to you when you're talking to pilots – but eventually you have to do it alone, of course. My instructors assured me that I'd had all the necessary preparation – I wasn't convinced. But in fact the whole thing happened almost without me realising it. I'd been so absorbed in what I was doing, it was only afterwards that I remembered no-one had been there checking up on me. So it was fine!

Interviewer: Bea asks what air controllers do when the weather's foggy.

Jake: Well, the airport's near a river so some days everything's covered in dense fog. Then the regular buzz of activity dies down, and there's just screens lighting up with windspeed reports and so on, which we still keep a close eye on. It doesn't mean we can relax completely – the fog can hang around for hours, or clear within minutes. We make the most of those times when we're not dealing with 50 planes an hour, though!

Interviewer: Now, a question from Richard – are you aware of how much people hate flight delays?

Jake: Well, controllers actually work to speed up flight departures, but I realise why people get frustrated when flights are running late. I know from experience, though, that it doesn't do any good. I do sometimes feel sorry for passengers, but the delay in departure schedules isn't something I let myself get concerned about up in the control tower. The departure times are decided according to the routes aircraft take, among other things. But that's hard to get that over to passengers.

Interviewer: Finally, I read that air traffic controllers recently helped out with an air display at the airport. How did that go?

Jake: Really well! We'd spent several months preparing for it. It was amazing how little disruption there was to flights. My job was talking to helicopter pilots filming the display, as well as monitoring other aircraft at the show. I hadn't expected to see quite such big crowds – it was certainly a satisfying feeling when it was over and nothing had gone wrong!

Interviewer: Thanks, Jake.

[pause]

Now you'll hear Part Four again.

tone

[The recording is repeated.]

[pause]

That's the end of Part Four.

There will now be a pause of five minutes for you to copy your answers onto the separate answer sheet. Be sure to follow the numbering of all the questions. I'll remind you when there's one minute left, so that you are sure to finish in time.

[Teacher, pause the recording here for five minutes. Remind students when they have one minute left.]

That's the end of the test. Please stop now. Your supervisor will now collect all the question papers and answer sheets.

Test 2 Key

Reading and Use of English (1 hour 15 minutes)

Part 1

1 D 2 B 3 A 4 B 5 D 6 C 7 A 8 D

Part 2

9 the **10** enough **11** it **12** whose **13** with **14** to **15** As **16** put

Part 3

17 intention **18** unwelcoming **19** citizens **20** satisfaction
21 competitive **22** strength **23** response **24** childish

Part 4

25 SHOULD be able / allowed | to come
26 was | an INCREASE in
27 the SUBJECT | every (single) / each
28 at | your DISPOSAL
29 has | (very/really) high EXPECTATIONS
30 didn't / did not REALISE | what

Part 5

31 A **32** C **33** D **34** B **35** B **36** C

Part 6

37 E **38** A **39** G **40** C **41** F **42** B

Part 7
43 D **44** A **45** B **46** A **47** C **48** A **49** C **50** B **51** C **52** D

Writing (1 hour 20 minutes)

Candidate responses are marked using the assessment scale on page 107-108.

Listening (approximately 40 minutes)

Part 1

1 B **2** A **3** B **4** B **5** B **6** C **7** A **8** A

Part 2

9 documentary **10** beauty **11** comet **12** moons
13 a space station **14** light (pollution) **15** (local) club
16 rings **17** discoveries **18** discipline

Part 3

19 H **20** A **21** G **22** C **23** D

Part 4

24 B **25** C **26** A **27** C **28** C **29** B **30** C

Transcript

This is the Cambridge English: First for Schools Listening Test. Test Two.

I'm going to give you the instructions for this test. I'll introduce each part of the test and give you time to look at the questions. At the start of each piece you'll hear this sound:

tone

You will hear each piece twice.

Remember, while you're listening, write your answers on the question paper. You'll have five minutes at the end of the test to copy your answers onto the separate answer sheet.

There will now be a pause. Please ask any questions now, because you must not speak during the test.

[pause]

Now open your question paper and look at Part One.

[pause]

PART 1

You'll hear people talking in eight different situations. For questions 1 to 8, choose the best answer (A, B or C).

Question 1 *You hear two friends talking about a lesson on the subject of newspapers.*

[pause]

tone

Girl: I enjoyed the discussion about newspapers. Having to do some research before the lesson meant we all knew what we had to discuss.

Boy: Yeah, but the discussion itself was a bit disorganised. We could've done with someone to lead it and make sure everyone had a chance to speak. We did get through a lot of topics though.

Girl: Everything from how newspapers deal with social media to the way they report on celebrities' private lives. I thought some people had some very interesting and different things to say.

Boy: Yeah, well, they talk as if they've got something new and amazing to tell you. I didn't hear anything I hadn't heard before, though.

[pause]

tone

[The recording is repeated.]

[pause]

Question 2 *You hear a man talking about skateboarders in the past.*

[pause]

tone

Man: I remember getting my first skateboard when I was 11. In those days skateboarders were generally seen as rebels who just did whatever they wanted without considering other people. So skateboarding was disapproved of by just about everyone, and people who did it liked to show off the fact that they were different. They had to practise in the streets because there weren't any specially built skateparks back then. But it's difficult to understand why they were so looked down on because I'm sure they didn't mean to get in the way of people and annoy them. It's completely different nowadays of course – you can practise in almost every city park.

[pause]

tone

[The recording is repeated.]

[pause]

Question 3 *You hear a girl talking about a diary she keeps.*

[pause]

tone

Girl: I've been writing a diary ever since my mother bought one for my seventh birthday, and I don't mean a book with dates for homework assignments and parties; for me it's more where I jot down my thoughts and feelings, and even sketch things that catch my eye. And I really appreciate being able to look back at what I've written. When I first began, I was worried my life was boring and there wouldn't be much to say, but it's actually made me realise that I do some quite cool stuff. Some people say writing a diary makes you remember the bad times. In fact, it's the opposite for me!

[pause]

tone

[The recording is repeated.]

[pause]

Question 4 *You hear a boy talking about a weekly video he posts online in which he expresses his opinions.*

[pause]

tone

Boy: I guess my videos have been a success, at least judging by the number of comments I get – sometimes there are so many I can't possibly answer them all. People who leave comments don't necessarily agree with every word I say and tell me why they think I'm wrong. I've learnt not to take this personally though. The thing is to get a discussion going if I can and arguing's part of that. There's a lot of pressure to come up with something new and fresh every week though, 'cos there are more people doing similar things to me, and it's important to keep everyone coming back for more.

[pause]

tone

[The recording is repeated.]

[pause]

Question 5 *You hear part of a programme about sea creatures called sea dragons.*

[pause]

tone

Man: Sea dragons may sound like mythical animals from a fairy tale, but they really do exist. They're amazing little creatures, close cousins of seahorses, and they feed off tiny fish and plankton. They don't have teeth or a stomach and, you know, they have to eat constantly, and they're able to travel quite long distances to find an adequate food supply. Until recently, scientists believed that there were only two species of sea dragon: the Leafy sea dragon, which has large plant like flaps flowing out of its body, and the Weedy sea dragon, which looks similar but has smaller flaps. It turns out there's a third type – one scientists have decided to call the Ruby sea dragon, thanks to its stunning colour.

[pause]

tone

[The recording is repeated.]

[pause]

Question 6 *You hear two friends talking about a film they've seen.*

[pause]

tone

Girl: Well, that film was rather disappointing, wasn't it?

Boy: I quite enjoyed it actually. More than the book it was based on. I didn't even manage to finish that. At least I know how the story ended now.

Girl: Well, actually the film totally changed the ending to the story, and I couldn't really understand why. And also, the boy who played the lead wasn't like I'd imagined – a bit too self-confident, you know?

Boy: But what did you think of the soundtrack? I found it a bit annoying and repetitive at times.

Girl: It's not the sort of thing you'd normally associate with that type of film – it seemed to work though.

[pause]

tone

[The recording is repeated.]

[pause]

Question 7 *You hear a news item about a small town in Alaska called Whittier.*

[pause]

tone

Woman: Whittier is a port in the US state of Alaska. When you get there you realize that there's something quite unusual about it. There are no picturesque little homes scattered around. Almost the only building you can see is the Begich Tower. This 14-storey complex is home to the majority of Whittier's 200 residents.

As well as providing accommodation, the Tower also houses Whittier's police station, supermarket and local government office. The school, which caters for kids of all ages, isn't too far from the building's west tower and is accessible via an underground tunnel. This means they've no excuse not to go even during Whittier's extremely severe winters.

[pause]

tone

[The recording is repeated.]

[pause]

Question 8 *You hear two friends talking about a dance competition.*

[pause]

tone

Boy: Are you looking forward to the dance competition on Saturday?

Girl: Yes. Are you going to go in for it?

Boy: No way. I'll buy a ticket and go and watch, though. What about you?

Girl: I'm actually competing in it – I'll probably be a bit nervous so I expect you'll have a better time than me.

Boy: Well, I'm sure you'll be fine and the audience will love it. But the people in charge really should've put it off until everyone knew what they were doing.

Girl: I could've done with more time to learn my steps, that's for sure!

[pause]

tone

[The recording is repeated.]

[pause]

That's the end of Part One.

Now turn to Part Two.

[pause]

PART 2

You'll hear an astronomer called Steve Mitchell talking about his work. For questions 9 to 18, complete the sentences with a word or short phrase.

You now have forty-five seconds to look at Part Two.

[pause]

tone

Steve: Hi. I'm Steve Mitchell and I work as an astronomer. I've been invited here today to tell you about my work.

I became keen on astronomy when I was a kid. I read science magazines intended for adults – anything about maths and physics – I didn't fully understand them but I loved the challenge. I watched a lot of TV – I loved nature programmes and I was also interested in a documentary that was popular then – that's what opened my eyes to the possibility of astronomy as a career.

As a teenager I went stargazing whenever I could. I didn't understand the complexity of everything I saw in the night sky at that stage – it was the beauty of it which appealed to me. It's easy to get excited by the mystery of the universe – there's still so much we don't know about it.

Every night felt like an adventure – I used to stay up late hoping to catch a glimpse of another galaxy through my telescope or to see a shooting star – what astronomers call a meteor. I didn't manage to spot one, unfortunately. I saw my first comet when I was sixteen though – that was thrilling, even for my family who weren't into astronomy.

Then I started studying the wide range of stars in the universe. Their different colours reflect how old they are. Recently I've taken a particular interest in all the different moons out there. There are millions of them orbiting the planets and it's astonishing that some are intensely hot and have volcanoes on their surface while others have an icy surface with oceans underneath.

I've recently been to a research centre in the USA and met other astronomers, which was something I'd always wanted to do. I also attended the launch of a spacecraft bound for Mars, which was awesome. One day it might be possible to live on a base there and lots of young scientists dream of doing that. Visiting a space station is definitely on the list of things I hope to do. And there are a couple orbiting the Earth right now!

Now, if you're thinking of taking up astronomy, don't worry about equipment. A good beginners' telescope isn't as expensive as you'd imagine. The weather can spoil things at times – you don't see stars in a sky covered with clouds, and light pollution is becoming an issue in cities. It may mean you see nothing, even on a cloudless night, which is often something people don't realise when they're starting out.

To get started in astronomy, you can learn the basics from a website – there are plenty to choose from. But that means you don't get to meet people and share ideas. You could consider taking a course, but a good one can be expensive. Joining a club is another option, and if you've got one locally that'd be the ideal thing.

So what should you try to spot first? Well, the planet Saturn is fascinating with its rings round it, which are clearly visible with a telescope, so it'd be good to look out for them. Jupiter has remarkably colourful clouds surrounding it, but they're not so easily seen. Another feature of Jupiter is what's known as its red spot, which is actually a huge storm in its atmosphere, but even experts struggle to locate it.

Astronomy, at a professional level, requires specialist knowledge and skills. Astronomers need to make calculations, for example, about the distance between stars. But amateur astronomers have a real part to play – teenagers have made significant discoveries including new stars, and there are certainly more to be made. So it's a worthwhile hobby!

To be a professional astronomer, you'll need a passion for the subject. Curiosity matters too – the ability to keep asking questions. And astronomy's a competitive career – so you'll need ambition. More than anything else, though, discipline is what's needed because all scientists have to be prepared to work hard.

[pause]

Now you'll hear Part Two again.

tone

[The recording is repeated.]

[pause]

That's the end of Part Two.

Now turn to Part Three.

[pause]

PART 3

You'll hear five short extracts in which teenagers are talking about a favourite book. For questions 19 to 23, choose from the list (A to H) what each speaker says about the book. Use the letters only once. There are three extra letters which you do not need to use.

You now have thirty seconds to look at Part Three.

[pause]

tone

Speaker 1

Girl: My favourite book's called 'Think Twice'. It's quite an old-fashioned book in some ways, but that's partly why it appeals to me, and also because my grandmother gave it to me. She said she used to love it when she was my age and she was so pleased when she found a copy of it for me. I haven't read anything else by the same writer but I'd like to. She presents the characters to you in a fascinating way which really brings them to life – and once you get into the plot, it keeps you guessing right to the end. It was adapted for television recently and they did it much better than I'd expected. But I still prefer the book.

[pause]

Speaker 2

Boy: I really love a book my brother gave me for my last birthday called 'Henry's Adventures'. He said the main character was just like me, which I think's a bit unfair because that guy, Henry, is always doing ridiculous things, getting into all sorts of trouble. The author's done a great job though, writing about the different places where Henry goes – I could almost see them! It's really hilarious – I just couldn't stop laughing, and I literally couldn't put the book down from the moment I picked it up. It'd make a great TV series. I've finished it now and I'm definitely going to read some other stuff by her.

[pause]

Speaker 3

Girl: I read lots when I'm on family holidays. We go to my grandparents who live near the sea, and I love lying on the beach with a good book. I particularly like books about other kids. The best one I read last summer was about a girl and her brother who suddenly had to move to the other end of the country. I could relate to it because we were just about to go through the same thing, so reading the book was good preparation for that. I have to say that it took me a little while to get into it, but I'm really glad I kept going.

[pause]

Speaker 4

Boy: There's a great series on TV at the moment about a boy who travels into space. I'd read the book that the series is based on and loved it. It's a lot funnier than the TV version, but they're both good in different ways. The hero's so like a friend of mine that the story could've been written about him, even down to the way the writer describes his appearance. My cousin asked to borrow it when I was staying at his place on a family holiday. He read the first page and didn't seem to be able to put it down again until he'd finished the whole thing.

[pause]

Speaker 5

Girl: I like stories about characters I can relate to. My favourite book's about a girl who lived in Ancient Rome. Although she lived at a very different time from me, many of the experiences she had are like ones that I've had too. It's an old book – my grandmother's name's in the front with the date 1950. She must've been about my age when she read it and it's great to think of her getting as much out of it back then as I do now. I love it even though it's quite a serious book – actually the writer's other books are much funnier.

[pause]

Now you'll hear Part Three again.

tone

[The recording is repeated.]

[pause]

That's the end of Part Three.

Now turn to Part Four.

[pause]

PART 4

You'll hear an interview with a man called Josh Reed, who teaches people how to climb trees. For questions 24 to 30, choose the best answer (A, B or C).

You now have one minute to look at Part Four.

[pause]

tone

Interviewer: Today Josh Reed, who runs courses teaching people to climb trees, will answer questions sent in by our listeners. But first Josh, how do people respond when you tell them what your job is?

Josh: They say things like: 'How can anyone do that?' It is a weird career choice, so I can understand why they don't believe anyone actually does it for a living. And it's certainly not the sort of work that would suit everyone.

Interviewer: Now, Ben, who's twelve, asks how old you were when you started climbing trees.

Josh: Well, I was about Ben's age actually. There were lots of trees where I lived, and I used to climb them after school. The world felt different from up there and it was an escape for me from all the homework and stuff I was expected to do. I began with the smaller trees, but soon progressed to the bigger, more difficult ones. I even climbed neighbours' trees. I'm sure my parents wouldn't have been very happy about that, but I just couldn't resist it.

Interviewer: Right. Chris, who's fifteen, asks if you've ever had any other jobs.

Josh: Well, I studied engineering at college, but there weren't many jobs in that field at the time. I saw an advert for an assistant tree surgeon, which involved making sure trees in parks and other public places were healthy and in good condition. So I went for the job and ended up doing it for fifteen years. I never had any formal qualifications, but I worked with people who knew a lot and passed their knowledge on to me. I should've given it up sooner than I did, though – I needed a new challenge.

Interviewer: That takes us to Elena's question: What made you want to start organising tree-climbing courses?

Josh: Well, working as a tree surgeon, you get to know a lot about things like different types of wood, how trees develop, and also their importance to us. It made me think about what we're doing to trees and nature generally. I reckoned if I encouraged people to climb trees, they might see the world from a different perspective and then become interested in protecting nature. Tree climbing makes you fit too, and I thought people might be attracted by that as well.

Interviewer: OK. Lucy asks if she could learn how to climb really tall trees.

Josh: There's lots of interest in them – like the Giant Redwoods which can be over a hundred metres high. With the safety equipment and methods, experts can get up them without injuring themselves. Their trunks tend to be quite plain, but there are birds, insects and small plants living at the top of them which, of course, people would like to get close to. But extremely tall trees are also extremely old and can be fragile, and they should be left alone as much as possible. There are plenty of others worth climbing.

Interviewer: Maria asks what sort of people you teach.

Josh: Well, the majority are just ordinary people. Actually, I've recently finished a course for some 15-year-olds. Teenagers sometimes get criticised for not paying attention to what instructors like me say. But this group were very attentive. Like younger people often do, they picked up the basic skills quite easily. The only real issue was when they climbed a tree with a huge ants' nest in it. Some of them got really worked up about that, but generally they were much more confident by the end.

Interviewer: Right. A final question from Peter. What are your plans for the future?

Josh: Actually, I'd like to continue to do interviews like this – they're a good way to get across the message about tree climbing. The gear we use is much better than it was and there are good techniques that can be passed on. Tree climbing doesn't have to be restricted to this country either. The idea that tree climbing is a good leisure activity to take up has plenty of potential in other places too, I'm sure.

Interviewer: OK Josh. Thanks very much.

[pause]

Now you'll hear Part Four again.

tone

[The recording is repeated.]

[pause]

That's the end of Part Four.

There will now be a pause of five minutes for you to copy your answers onto the separate answer sheet. Be sure to follow the numbering of all the questions. I'll remind you when there's one minute left, so that you are sure to finish in time.

[Teacher, pause the recording here for five minutes. Remind students when they have one minute left.]

That's the end of the test. Please stop now. Your supervisor will now collect all the question papers and answer sheets.

Test 3 Key

Reading and Use of English (1 hour 15 minutes)

Part 1

1 D **2** B **3** C **4** A **5** B **6** C **7** D **8** A

Part 2

9 what **10** who **11** at **12** Since **13** spends **14** take
15 with **16** have/enjoy

Part 3

17 disappears **18** mysterious **19** explanation **20** active
21 steadily **22** unable **23** depth **24** surrounding

Part 4

25 no USE | asking
26 WISH I'd / I had | remembered OR WISH I had not / hadn't | forgotten
27 me OFF | for
28 I'm / I am | UNFAMILIAR with
29 were / had been EXPECTED | to turn/show
30 OUGHT to | have told

Part 5

31 A **32** B **33** A **34** D **35** C **36** A

Part 6

37 D **38** G **39** C **40** E **41** A **42** F

Part 7

43 B **44** D **45** C **46** A **47** A **48** C **49** B **50** D **51** B **52** A

Writing (1 hour 20 minutes)

Candidate responses are marked using the assessment scale on page 107-108.

Listening (approximately 40 minutes)

Part 1

1 B **2** B **3** A **4** A **5** C **6** A **7** B **8** A

Part 2

9 rules **10** sleeping(-)bag **11** attitude **12** sand(-)storms
13 dried(-)fruit(s) **14** check(-)points **15** (sun)(-)glasses
16 sunsets **17** (extra) clothes **18** camels

Part 3

19 F **20** B **21** E **22** D **23** G

Part 4

24 C **25** C **26** A **27** B **28** A **29** B **30** A

Transcript

This is the Cambridge English: First for Schools Listening Test. Test Three.

I'm going to give you the instructions for this test. I'll introduce each part of the test and give you time to look at the questions. At the start of each piece you'll hear this sound:

tone

You will hear each piece twice.

Remember, while you're listening, write your answers on the question paper. You'll have five minutes at the end of the test to copy your answers onto the separate answer sheet.

There will now be a pause. Please ask any questions now, because you must not speak during the test.

[pause]

Now open your question paper and look at Part One.

[pause]

PART 1 *You'll hear people talking in eight different situations. For questions 1 to 8, choose the best answer (A, B or C).*

Question 1 *You hear part of an interview with a tennis player after a match.*

[pause]

tone

Man: How do you think you played?

Woman: Not my best, but I still beat a top player. In that sense, it was satisfactory.

Man: Are you still recovering from the knee operation you had?

Woman: Yes, but I can't let that affect me in a tough game. I have to push myself all the way. I'm pleased my knee feels like it's back to normal – much of that's down to the doctors and physiotherapists who treated me. I really owe them a lot.

Man: Most of the crowd today wanted your opponent to win. What did that feel like?

Woman: She was the home player, so their positive reaction to her was natural. It's something players get used to.

[pause]

tone

[The recording is repeated.]

[pause]

Question 2 *You hear two friends talking about a comedy show they went to see.*

[pause]

tone

Man: Gerry King was great last night, wasn't he?

Woman: Yes, he's even funnier live than he is on TV. And he had plenty of jokes I'd never heard before.

Man: He does tend to stick to certain topics – people he meets, problems he has, you know – he is extremely funny though. Most people there were obviously big fans of his.

Woman: Well, he's not rude or aggressive like some comedians. I think that's why people responded to him so well. The atmosphere was great, even though we were in a stadium, which seemed rather a strange place for comedy.

Man: It depends on the size of the crowd. There's plenty of humour at big football matches.

[pause]

tone

[The recording is repeated.]

[pause]

Question 3 *You hear part of a radio phone-in programme about cycling in cities.*

[pause]

tone

Woman: Our next caller is Marek. What's your point, Marek?

Man: Well, you've had some callers talking about annoying things cyclists do – like riding through traffic lights when they're red, or going on pavements and bothering pedestrians. What these callers didn't say is that cyclists do these things because the traffic and roads in this city are often unsafe for cycling. Would they do these things if there were more lanes set aside for them? I doubt it. The benefits cycling brings are obvious, which is why so many people are starting to do it. What we should be doing is making it easier and safer for them rather than finding fault with them.

[pause]

tone

[The recording is repeated.]

[pause]

Question 4 *You hear two friends discussing an article about junk food.*

[pause]

tone

Girl: Have you read this article about junk food?

Boy: No. What does it say?

Girl: It's about how food companies invest an incredible amount of money designing junk food so it's cheap, easy to eat, and makes us want to eat more of it. It's difficult to believe they're allowed to do that when you think how bad it is for us.

Boy: The trouble with reports like that is that they're giving unpopular news, so people tend to ignore them. Just think what our friends are like.

Girl: Most of them would rather not know. I'm determined to give up certain things, though, even though I might not find it easy to.

[pause]

tone

[The recording is repeated.]

[pause]

Question 5 *You hear a teacher talking about a large picture her students are painting to be displayed.*

[pause]

tone

Woman: Right, everyone. You're going to get together as a class this week to paint a picture that'll be on the wall in the school entrance – so it has to be good. It'll feature local landmarks – we'll research these in more detail later on this term. Now, the reason for doing this is to provide inspiration that'll support your schoolwork, because you can't come up with interesting ideas or write great stories if you haven't had the chance to use your imagination. So, I hope you're all feeling motivated to produce great artwork – 'cos the plan is to have this completed before the end of next week!

[pause]

tone

[The recording is repeated.]

[pause]

Question 6 *You hear a boy telling a friend about a trip he went on with his father.*

[pause]

tone

Girl: How was your trip with your dad?

Boy: Well, we'd never gone off on our own and done anything like that before and I really saw a different side to him. I couldn't believe he'd actually looked online and booked the perfect place for us to stay – super-modern, not really his thing – he just knew it'd be completely mine. That was kind of him. And he'd planned loads of things for us to do – I don't know when he found the time because he's usually so busy. But Dad's always been into exploring new places – and that's what we did!

Girl: You get on really well with your dad, don't you?

Boy: Yeah.

[pause]

tone

[The recording is repeated.]

[pause]

Question 7 *You hear a girl talking about a science experiment at her school.*

[pause]

tone

Girl: We did a really cool science experiment at school yesterday, involving loads of plastic bottles with water in them, which we used to design and make rockets that would actually fly! The science was all a bit complicated for us really, even after our teacher had explained the theory behind it in detail. But we fired the rockets from a launch pad on the playing field, and they reached quite a height – we didn't manage that when we practised the day before! Mind you, they showered everyone with water as they went up, including our teacher! But no-one really seemed to mind. It was great fun.

[pause]

tone

[The recording is repeated.]

[pause]

Question 8 *You hear two friends discussing an experiment into the effects of spending time in space.*

[pause]

tone

Woman: Tell me about that experiment you were reading about.

Man: I'm going to see what else has been posted online actually, but basically six researchers who hardly knew each other volunteered to be shut away in a kind of capsule – they had to stay in it for a year without fresh air or fresh food.

Woman: And the point was … ?

Man: To see what effect that would have on their bodies … and their minds. I certainly wouldn't be brave enough to do that!

Woman: Well, they wouldn't come to much harm, would they? You've got me wanting to find out what happened to them now.

[pause]

tone

[The recording is repeated.]

[pause]

That's the end of Part One.

Now turn to Part Two.

[pause]

PART 2

You'll hear an interview with a boy called Luke Tyler, who took part in a desert marathon race. For questions 9 to 18, complete the sentences with a word or short phrase.

You now have forty-five seconds to look at Part Two.

[pause]

tone

Luke: My name's Luke Tyler and I'm going to talk about a tough sporting event I took part in – the Marathon of the Sands, an annual six-day race across the desert! The distance covered is more or less 250 kilometres, but the routes differ from one year to the next and aren't announced until the day before. However, the rules competitors follow have remained unchanged since the race started back in 1986.

Almost everything I needed had to fit into a backpack. And I had to think carefully about the weight I was carrying – most things I'd decided to take were fairly light anyway, such as my compass to keep me going the right way. I checked the sleeping bag I'd chosen was as light as possible, though. My small cooker to heat up food was obviously heavier – but to me that was essential!

You obviously need to be fit to take on a huge challenge like this, so I spent the months before setting off doing intensive training. This preparation was vital, but at the end of the day, attitude counted for more – just knowing I could do it. I got advice from friends, though it wasn't as useful as I'd hoped because they'd never attempted running anything as hard as a desert marathon.

Before taking on this challenge, I was aware that there were dangers in the desert. We were warned about scorpions, for example, but I wasn't too bothered about those. The sandstorms concerned me more because they can appear out of nowhere. The heat I was prepared for, which was a good thing, because sometimes the temperature reached 40 degrees!

The race organisers were very concerned for our welfare. They insisted that each runner consumed 4,000 calories a day, although how you did that was up to you. I tended to get my nutrition from dried meat. They'd suggested dried fruit too, though I didn't take as much of that as I should've done. I couldn't resist snacking on biscuits, which I don't suppose was officially recommended!

The length of the race means it's exhausting. I was always looking forward to the breaks. These opportunities come along every few kilometres at what they call checkpoints and they're welcome sights for weary runners. They're basically just stop-off places where shade and water are provided, and information about the next stage.

Thinking of comfort during the race, I wore trainers that were slightly big for me and got some serious blisters. There was a medical team who were brilliant at treating sore feet, but luckily I'd taken plenty of plasters with me, so didn't need their help. There was also a danger of damage to your eyes from the bright light, so I'd gone for sunglasses that cut out the glare. They certainly made life more bearable.

The desert was beautiful. There were some stunning mountains in the background, and we ran through some interesting villages too. At night, the sky was so dark that the stars were just amazing, and the sunsets seemed more beautiful than any I'd seen back home – they're what'll stick in my memory.

After a couple of days, I looked in my bag and realised there were some items that weren't strictly necessary. I was told it'd be cold at night so I'd taken extra clothes with me. But the tent I slept in was cosy, so I got rid of them. I considered dumping some of the fuel I used for cooking, but in the end kept it. And I managed to lose my sun-cream, so I just borrowed some from another runner.

I was never on my own. Volunteers along the way helped to make sure things went smoothly. Several camels not far behind us were transporting heavy camping equipment, and I sometimes looked up to see a couple of helicopters following us to check on our well-being. That was reassuring. And there were also several trucks full of reporters and camera equipment.

It was an unforgettable experience and one I would …

[pause]

Now you'll hear Part Two again.

[The recording is repeated.]

[pause]

That's the end of Part Two.

Now turn to Part Three.

[pause]

PART 3

You'll hear five short extracts in which teenagers are talking about what's called a survival course, where they learnt the skills you need to live in a forest. For questions 19 to 23, choose from the list (A to H) how each speaker felt during the course. Use the letters only once. There are three extra letters which you do not need to use.

You now have thirty seconds to look at Part Three.

[pause]

tone

Speaker 1

Girl: I spent three days with some students in my class at a place in a forest where they teach you how to survive in the wild. We learnt how to make an open fire – it was great they allowed us to do that. Everything was done in groups – which makes sense, I suppose. I was with people who had very different ideas from me, though we got on well. I really fancied going fishing but our group never got round to doing that, which I was quite upset about, actually. We did spend a whole day building a shelter out of branches and leaves – it was really hard work, but we slept in it too, which was great fun.

[pause]

Speaker 2

Boy: My class went away for a weekend to learn skills we'd need if we ever got lost in a rainforest, or something like that. For example, our instructor showed us how to purify river water and make it drinkable by pouring it through a cloth. We did it very carefully, but the water still looked a strange colour. I did drink some even though I was quite worried it might make me sick. Before we went, I thought we might struggle on the course because we had to work in groups and some kids in my class don't really get on. But we made a good fire – my friend Joe eventually managed to light it by knocking two stones together – he was so proud of that.

[pause]

Speaker 3

Girl: I signed up for the survival skills course – my friends were going and I was excited to be able to spend some time with them. But the weather was terrible and I was miserable because I ended up getting a cold. The instructor said it was too wet to make fires, but we did other things. One day, she took us on a long walk through the forest and then left us to find our way back. Luckily, one of the boys in the group worked out a route back through the forest to the campsite – it was really hard and I don't know how he did it. I'd never been in a situation like that before, and to be honest it wasn't the best thing I'd ever done.

[pause]

Speaker 4

Boy: I thought doing the survival skills course with a group of friends from school would be something I'd really enjoy – I ended up learning a lot too. It didn't start very well because I had a bad headache the first day, but fortunately it went away. We did lots of different activities. For example, our instructor showed us things in the forest that you can eat and he also taught us how to use natural materials to make things. I struggled with that, though. I mean, we spent a whole day carving wood and my friends made three different tools but I only made one simple spoon, which was very annoying and I did feel a bit upset about it. But everything else was great!

[pause]

Speaker 5

Girl: I really appreciated the survival skills weekend. The activities were in groups and we did different things like learning how to live off nature – what plants you can eat, and which would make you sick if you tried them. One afternoon we had a race in groups to make a raft out of tree trunks. Then we had to use it to get from one side of a river to the other. I'd never done anything like that before and it did seem a bit strange, but I was really glad they gave me the chance to have a go. We didn't get to track wild animals, which was something our instructor promised we'd do, but I didn't mind because I'll definitely go back there again.

[pause]

Now you'll hear Part Three again.

tone

[The recording is repeated.]

[pause]

That's the end of Part Three.

Now turn to Part Four.

[pause]

PART 4

You'll hear an interview with a man called Danny Taylor, who is a record producer with his own recording studio. For questions 24 to 30, choose the best answer (A, B or C).

You now have one minute to look at Part Four.

[pause]

tone

Interviewer: Today we're talking to a record producer, Danny Taylor. Welcome Danny. You set up your own recording studio when you were 20. Why did you do that?

Danny: I used to play keyboards in a number of different bands. I also wrote songs and recorded a few with the idea of making an album. But studio time was getting too expensive, and I thought that if I had my own place, I could get my material done cheaply – as well as getting other professional musicians to pay me for recording their stuff. I didn't have any experience of working for a record company – but I bought some equipment and gave it a try.

Interviewer: You've had the studio for ten years now. Do you make a good living from it?

Danny: It's still a small business, but I've produced records for well-known bands, and I'm quite well-established. The music industry has changed considerably over the years and I've obviously had to adapt to survive – I don't just record pop music anymore. I do what might sound like interesting work, recording music for cartoons and adverts, which helps me keep the studio going. It's a bit of a pain actually though – because I'd much rather focus on the sort of music I'm into.

Interviewer: You've had mixed reactions to the location of your new studio, haven't you?

Danny: Well, recording studios generally tend to be in big cities – places where there's lots going on – good transport connections, shops, and so on. If that's the environment people are looking for – many musicians are – then my studio out in the country wouldn't be the ideal place for them. But many up-and-coming groups and solo artists see the sense in being free of distractions, so they can concentrate on creating high-quality recordings.

Interviewer: Some rock musicians have a reputation for bad behaviour. Do you see any of that?

Danny: You get all these press stories about famous musicians causing trouble. I'm not saying it doesn't happen, but people come to the studio to work. Recording's an intense activity and there are times when the singer has a different opinion from the guitarist, for example, and things do get a bit heated – that's only to be expected. But it's good that musicians have strong emotions because all that comes out in the music they produce.

Interviewer: Would you say your job's hard?

Danny: It can be. With famous artists there are so many things I have to do to please them before they'll get down to work. Then there are musicians who ask me to improve their songs. Sometimes they just don't have what it takes, though – I have to be honest about that, which is particularly unpleasant. And new bands send in home recordings of tracks they'd like me to record professionally – I'm so busy I can seldom listen to them all, which is a shame because I'm sure I miss some good stuff.

Interviewer: Are there aspects of music production you're particularly good at?

Danny: Producers vary. Some are great at the technical stuff; some, like me, are good at arranging music; others can tell whether something they've written will be a commercial success or not. I think what bands appreciate, though, is the sounds I produce and the fact that my productions stand out from other stuff on the market. Personally, I get a lot of pleasure working with younger musicians – they're open to new ideas and it's satisfying to see how they develop.

Interviewer: Finally, what advice would you give to a young person interested in going into music production?

Danny: Um … many colleges run courses, and give the impression that there are plenty of jobs available for people who do them, which isn't necessarily the case. As recording technology gets easier to use, more musicians are looking into producing music themselves and buying some quite sophisticated equipment to do it. The only people who should consider making a career out of it though, are those who're really prepared to dedicate time and energy to it. But if you're ready for that, then music production is brilliant.

Interviewer: OK Danny. Thanks.

[pause]

Now you'll hear Part Four again.

[The recording is repeated.]

[pause]

That's the end of Part Four.

There will now be a pause of five minutes for you to copy your answers onto the separate answer sheet. Be sure to follow the numbering of all the questions. I'll remind you when there's one minute left, so that you are sure to finish in time.

[Teacher, pause the recording here for five minutes. Remind students when they have one minute left.]

That's the end of the test. Please stop now. Your supervisor will now collect all the question papers and answer sheets.

Test 4 Key

Reading and Use of English (1 hour 15 minutes)

Part 1

1 B 2 A 3 C 4 D 5 B 6 D 7 A 8 C

Part 2

9 to **10** be **11** it **12** like **13** had **14** are **15** on **16** which

Part 3

17 calculation **18** increasingly **19** irresponsible **20** produced
21 consideration **22** environmentally **23** unpredictable
24 consumers

Part 4

25 wish it WOULD | stop
26 PUT you | off
27 the BEST of | my
28 to be | a SIGNIFICANT reduction
29 no MATTER | how hard/much I
30 TALK you into | helping

Part 5

31 C **32** D **33** A **34** B **35** B **36** B

Part 6

37 G **38** B **39** E **40** D **41** A **42** F

Part 7

43 C **44** B **45** C **46** B **47** A **48** B **49** D **50** A
51 D **52** A

Writing (1 hour 20 minutes)

Candidate responses are marked using the assessment scale on page 107-108.

Listening (approximately 40 minutes)

Part 1

1 B **2** C **3** B **4** A **5** A **6** B **7** C **8** B

Part 2

9 shop(-)assistant **10** wave(-)makers **11** challenge **12** stand (up)
13 emotional **14** practice **15** weather **16** space
17 adaptable **18** photography

Part 3

19 F **20** E **21** A **22** B **23** H

Part 4

24 A **25** C **26** A **27** B **28** A **29** B **30** C

Transcript

This is the Cambridge English: First for Schools Listening Test. Test Four.

I'm going to give you the instructions for this test. I'll introduce each part of the test and give you time to look at the questions. At the start of each piece you'll hear this sound:

tone

You will hear each piece twice.

Remember, while you're listening, write your answers on the question paper. You'll have five minutes at the end of the test to copy your answers onto the separate answer sheet.

There will now be a pause. Please ask any questions now, because you must not speak during the test.

[pause]

Now open your question paper and look at Part One.

[pause]

PART 1 *You'll hear people talking in eight different situations. For questions 1 to 8, choose the best answer (A, B or C).*

Question 1 *You hear two friends talking about a pop band they saw on TV.*

[pause]

tone

Boy: That programme last night about that new pop group was cool, wasn't it?

Girl: I know. I'd seen online that their average age was about sixteen, so I was really interested to see them!

Boy: What I hadn't realised was that the youngest one's only twelve. And they've had sell-out concerts all over the country. You wouldn't believe that for a new band, would you?

Girl: I think people can be successful however old they are – the fact they've done so well when they've only been around for six months does make them unusual though.

Boy: Their singing's quite impressive too, don't you think?

Girl: Well, the lead singer's great anyway!

[pause]

tone

[The recording is repeated.]

[pause]

Question 2 *You hear part of an interview with a scientist.*

[pause]

tone

Man: A handful of schools have been taking part in research to discover if there are any benefits for teenagers in starting classes later – at around ten or even ten-thirty in the morning. It wasn't easy to persuade the schools to get involved because people are understandably sceptical about changing timetables and the disruption that might be caused. Studies carried out in the last six months have suggested that teenagers feel more alert and focused later in the morning, but little practical action has been taken so far. It seems that changing the hours of the school day could have a radical effect on the well-being and the academic performance of teenagers though.

[pause]

tone

[The recording is repeated.]

[pause]

Question 3 *You hear a teacher talking to a student about doing homework.*

[pause]

tone

Boy: Did you want to speak to me?

Woman: Yes, Sam. You said you've been finding it hard to get through all your homework and sometimes you end up finishing it late at night. And you said you were thinking of giving up other things you do after school, like basketball or guitar lessons. The thing is, taking a bit of time out from your schoolwork each day isn't such a bad idea. What I would say is, if you have several homework tasks, tackle the most challenging ones while you're still reasonably fresh. Then, once that's done, have a little rest before moving on to the other things you need to do.

[pause]

tone

[The recording is repeated.]

[pause]

Question 4 *You hear a football fan talking about his team.*

[pause]

tone

Man: When your team's just lost five games in a row, you've got to ask questions. The easy thing to do is to blame the manager, and say the decisions he's made and the way he's set the team up to play are responsible for the mess they're in. I'm fed up with hearing that excuse. The players just look out of condition. I mean, they seem worn out by the end of the first half. Mental attitude in sport is important too, of course, and they do seem to have more motivation than last season, when they were just wandering around the pitch looking as if they'd lost before they'd even started.

[pause]

tone

[The recording is repeated.]

[pause]

Question 5 *You hear a film critic talking about a film for teenagers.*

[pause]

tone

Woman: The film, 'Olaf the Mighty', is a fantasy as spectacular as the popular novel of the same name, from which it's been adapted. At one point, several of the actors turn into monsters right in front of your eyes. The film was worth seeing just for that. As for the characters, they certainly have the looks – though the same can't be said about the acting. The male lead played by Rob Weedon is obviously supposed to be the hero, but he comes across as weak. In fact, you want the bad guy to beat him, because the relatively unknown actor playing him gives an impressive and more convincing performance.

[pause]

tone

[The recording is repeated.]

[pause]

Question 6 *You hear two teenagers discussing a visit to a zoo.*

[pause]

tone

Boy: We went to Chester Zoo last week. There were several areas that've been turned into copies of islands in south-east Asia – zoos seem to have some unusual ways of getting us to visit!

Girl: They'll do anything to get more visitors in – it's about the money really.

Boy: They aren't just about that, though. They've got an important part to play in protecting endangered species.

Girl: Preserving creatures in their natural habitat would be in the animals' best interests though. Still, they do inform us about wildlife we wouldn't otherwise see.

Boy: So you admit there's some point to zoos then: that they at least raise awareness of the natural world.

Girl: But do you really think they're necessary …

[pause]

tone

[The recording is repeated.]

[pause]

Question 7 *You hear a young professional ballet dancer talking about performing.*

[pause]

tone

Woman: Because I'm so young and attracting attention, there's the pressure that comes from everyone watching your every move, looking for what you've done wrong and pulling your performance to pieces. This holds back some dancers – they just freeze. But I find that other people's expectations spur me on to achieve more. By nature, I'm quite shy, and certainly when I'm practising in the studio I am rather self-conscious. On stage though, I feel at home. I can understand when other girls confide in me about having problems with nerves, but I feel so sure of myself in front of the audience that it's not something I've personally experienced.

[pause]

tone

[The recording is repeated.]

[pause]

Question 8 *You hear a teacher talking about the history of the refrigerator.*

[pause]

tone

Man: The technology to chill food first became available in the mid-nineteenth century. It seems such a ground-breaking and life-changing idea that it's perhaps surprising that few people initially saw the benefit of it. This was because the first domestic fridges were incredibly expensive and it was a good deal cheaper to cut natural ice from lakes and use that instead. However, as supermarkets became popular and people stopped going shopping for fresh food every day, the popularity of fridges increased. The invention of the fridge certainly changed people's eating habits forever, but the claim that it was as important a technological breakthrough as other inventions from the same period needs to be questioned.

[pause]

tone

[The recording is repeated.]

[pause]

That's the end of Part One.

Now turn to Part Two.

[pause]

PART 2

You'll hear a man called Jack Morton talking about his job as a windsurfing instructor. For questions 9 to 18, complete the sentences with a word or short phrase.

You now have forty-five seconds to look at Part Two.

[pause]

tone

Jack: I'm Jack Morton, and I work as a windsurfing instructor. I'm here to answer questions from listeners about how to turn your love of watersports into a possible career in the future.

First, Simon asks whether I went into watersports in order to become an instructor. Well, when I left school, I actually studied to be a journalist, but soon discovered that wasn't for me. I managed to get taken on as a shop assistant, which meant I had plenty of free time to do watersports, and I ended up taking a sailing instructors' course. And that's where it began!

Now Bethany asks how I got my current job. Well, after I'd built up experience in sailing, I applied to a company called Outdoorlife – they specialise in watersports holidays. I'd seen their brochure, and I fell in love with the pictures of windsurfers blasting across the lake. I didn't join them in the end, but was lucky enough to find work with a smaller company called Wavemakers, and I'm still with them.

John asks what I particularly like about windsurfing. Well, I've done a bit of waterskiing, you know – the excitement of that sport is certainly very appealing and it requires a lot of skill. For me, though, nothing beats windsurfing, for the challenge of it.

Gillian asks what kind of students I prefer to teach – total beginners or more experienced windsurfers. Well, I love both, but I suppose the really satisfying thing is when you see people who've never been on a windsurfing board before, finally mastering how to stand up on one. Doing that on water isn't easy. It's also pleasing, of course, when someone picks up the basics and actually manages to change direction, for example!

Of course, the majority of people are thrilled just to have a go, but one or two get quite emotional when they actually get the hang of it. They may have felt pressured if other members of the group seemed to be doing better than them. Ideally, people should feel relaxed about the whole thing 'cos it's supposed to be fun.

And obviously there's a lot to learn when you first start windsurfing. People often think sheer strength is what's required to get moving fast across the water, and that may be true to a certain extent. A good technique helps, of course, but with practice, I'd say anyone can succeed, and in fact that's all that's needed unless you want to be a professional!

Ben asks what mistakes students make when they're windsurfing. Well, as they get better, they worry about having the right equipment, then they really start pushing themselves hard, spending more and more time out on the lake. When they're out there, they don't pay enough attention to the weather, though – things can change very quickly and they need to be aware of that.

Also, I've noticed windsurfers often seem to crowd together in the same small stretch of lake – I can't understand why they do that! It's like people who park right next to one another in a car park, when they're the only two vehicles there! You really need to allow other surfers space and they should do the same for you – otherwise you can soon get into difficulty.

Sandra asks what skills you need to do this job. Well, it really involves being well-organised – knowing who's coming when and what everyone's capable of – I suppose that's true of many jobs. My boss has always commented positively on how adaptable I am – changing my schedule at short notice, that kind of thing. That all makes for a supportive working environment.

Finally, some people have asked about other career possibilities related to watersports. Obviously having qualifications is useful whatever you decide to do. Increasingly, people are being asked to demonstrate that they're good at photography, and if you combine that with watersports, it can lead to a very interesting career. And, of course, marketing skills are useful these days too, and offer another career route.

[pause]

Now you'll hear Part Two again.

[The recording is repeated.]

[pause]

That's the end of Part Two.

Now turn to Part Three.

[pause]

PART 3

You'll hear five short extracts in which teenagers are remembering the day they met their best friend for the first time. For questions 19 to 23, choose from the list (A to H) how each speaker felt on that day. Use the letters only once. There are three extra letters which you do not need to use.

You now have thirty seconds to look at Part Three.

[pause]

tone

Speaker 1

Girl: My best friend's Alice. I met her the day we moved into the flat next door to hers. Alice's mum sent her round to see if we needed any help. My mum was a bit worried because there was stuff all over the place, but she did think it was nice that our new neighbours were welcoming and seemed keen to find out if we were settling in OK. Anyway, Alice and I were just having a chat when we noticed her cat strolling into our house and making itself at home. We couldn't help laughing about it and right then we knew we were going to get along.

[pause]

Speaker 2

Boy: My best friend's Jake and we're in the same class at school – we met on our first day there, which was great because I'd been worried that I might not make any friends. It was brilliant when Jake asked if I'd like to go round to his place after school. That was four years ago, and we've been inseparable ever since. We've recently got into tennis so we spend a lot of time practising and we go to tournaments most weekends. We always seem to find the same things funny too. Jake says it's a shame we didn't meet at primary school really, and I agree.

[pause]

Speaker 3

Girl: Maria's definitely my best friend. My mum met her mum at work and they had a lot in common, so Mum invited the whole family over. I was really interested to see what Maria was like. I'd just got a new computer game that I thought she'd enjoy playing. So it was a real let-down when she wouldn't even give it a try – she made it clear that she wasn't into computer games and suggested watching a film instead. Mum said Maria was the guest so I had to put up with it. I wasn't too pleased about that, so our first meeting was a bit awkward. Fortunately, things have looked up since then.

[pause]

Speaker 4

Boy: Ben moved into the empty flat next to ours three years ago. I was dying to know who'd be living next door, hoping there'd be someone my age. I stood at the window watching as our new neighbours unloaded their stuff from the removal van. I felt a bit uncomfortable when Ben caught sight of me watching him! But it was great to see that he was carrying in a games console identical to mine – I went out to introduce myself! Ben told me he'd been a bit scared about going to a new school and was relieved to discover I was going there too. We've been best friends ever since.

[pause]

Speaker 5

Girl: Emily's my cousin, but she's also my best friend. I didn't meet her till I was 12, which may seem a bit unusual but that was because she'd been living in Japan up till then. I was a bit concerned about meeting her and wasn't sure I wanted to, because I couldn't imagine why she'd be interested in someone like me. But I was keen to find out about everything she'd done before coming to the UK and we hit it off straight away. She's really good fun and always makes me laugh when we're out together. Actually we feel a bit put out if we go too long without seeing each other.

[pause]

Now you'll hear Part Three again.

tone

[The recording is repeated.]

[pause]

That's the end of Part Three.

Now turn to Part Four.

[pause]

PART 4

You'll hear an interview with a young artist called Martin Gold, who is learning how to draw the cartoon stories that appear in magazines. For questions 24 to 30, choose the best answer (A, B or C).

You now have one minute to look at Part Four.

[pause]

tone

Interviewer: I'm with Martin Gold, an artist who's learning how to draw cartoons for a living. Martin, what a cool job! How did you get started in it?

Martin: My dad's a graphic designer, and obviously drawing skills are important for him – and he expected me to share his enthusiasm, getting me to copy his funny little sketches! Then, like all kids, I started to buy comics – you know magazines full of cartoon stories. But what caught my attention and appealed to me was the images rather than the stories they were telling – that got me wanting to be creative and see what unusual ideas I could come up with.

Interviewer: So, how did your school react when you told them what job you wanted to do?

Martin: I can't say they were encouraging! My art teacher admitted I'd probably find work, but she still tried to persuade me to look into other possibilities involving drawing – like fashion design. That sounded to me like something it'd be incredibly hard to get into – not at all what I wanted! I was aware though that, as a cartoonist, I wouldn't be guaranteed regular work. But I was determined to stick with it.

Interviewer: So you didn't give up ...

Martin: No – if there was an event at school or if the local drama club was putting on a show at a local theatre I'd do the posters, and they went down incredibly well – I hadn't expected that and I needed that approval. Later on though, when I sent stuff I'd done off to magazines, the replies I got were mixed. Although one or two did praise my work, nobody wanted to publish it. I started to question whether I'd ever succeed in a career in art.

Interviewer: And then you went to Barcelona for the summer. What effect did that have?

Martin: Oh, amazing. I'd gone there hoping to do a drawing course with a cartoonist who has a different and very interesting approach. Unfortunately, that was cancelled at the last minute, but I'd bought my plane ticket so I still went. I spent my time sketching different sights in the city, and that did improve my drawing skills. Somehow, just being there was enough – I came home brimming with new ideas from everything I'd seen and heard. After that my artwork seemed to have a new purpose!

Interviewer: So, then you went on to art school and started experimenting with new ways of drawing cartoons. Did you enjoy that?

Martin: Yeah, up till then I'd been drawing using big marker pens, 'cos they made really strong lines on the paper. But there I was introduced to Indian ink, which I was told some experienced cartoonists prefer. I could see why – people who are used to working with it can get far more differences in shading and line thickness into their drawings. The more immediate effect for me was that I could turn out finished drawings more rapidly than before. I guess eventually I'll learn to make better use of it and start to introduce more characters into my drawings too.

Interviewer: You're currently working as a 'ghost artist' for a newspaper. What's that exactly?

Martin: Well, I'm called in when one of their usual cartoonists is unavailable, for whatever reason. My drawings have to look identical to what would normally appear. The work's giving me a real insight into the world of cartoonists – more than I thought it would, but it's getting in the way of what I really want to do. So, I won't do it forever, but it pays the bills for now.

Interviewer: So, have you got the qualities needed to succeed as a cartoonist?

Martin: Well, I don't always feel particularly inspired. But you still have to try and produce the goods 'cos so many people are depending on you. It'll be hard, but I reckon I've got the determination. I was talking to my boss and he was saying how important it is for a cartoonist to be focussed and to have a methodical way of doing things. I'm a bit concerned 'cos that doesn't sound like me! I'm just hoping he's wrong – that there's more than one way to get the job done!

[pause]

Now you'll hear Part Four again.

[The recording is repeated.]

[pause]

That's the end of Part Four.

There will now be a pause of five minutes for you to copy your answers onto the separate answer sheet. Be sure to follow the numbering of all the questions. I'll remind you when there's one minute left, so that you are sure to finish in time.

[Teacher, pause the recording here for five minutes. Remind students when they have one minute left.]

That's the end of the test. Please stop now. Your supervisor will now collect all the question papers and answer sheets.

CAMBRIDGE ENGLISH
Language Assessment
Part of the University of Cambridge

Do not write in this box

SAMPLE

Candidate Name
If not already printed, write name in CAPITALS and complete the Candidate No. grid (in pencil).

Candidate Signature

Examination Title

Centre

Supervisor:
If the candidate is ABSENT or has WITHDRAWN shade here

Centre No.

Candidate No.

Examination Details

Candidate Answer Sheet

Instructions

Use a PENCIL (B or HB).

Rub out any answer you wish to change using an eraser.

Parts 1, 5, 6 and 7:
Mark ONE letter for each question.

For example, if you think **B** is the right answer to the question, mark your answer sheet like this:

0 A B C D

Parts 2, 3 and 4:
Write your answer clearly in CAPITAL LETTERS.

For Parts 2 and 3 write one letter in each box. For example:

0 EXAMPLE

Part 1

1	A	B	C	D
2	A	B	C	D
3	A	B	C	D
4	A	B	C	D
5	A	B	C	D
6	A	B	C	D
7	A	B	C	D
8	A	B	C	D

Part 2

		Do not write below here
9		9 1 0 u
10		10 1 0 u
11		11 1 0 u
12		12 1 0 u
13		13 1 0 u
14		14 1 0 u
15		15 1 0 u
16		16 1 0 u

Continues over →

Part 3

		Do not write below here
17		17 1 0 u
18		18 1 0 u
19		19 1 0 u
20		20 1 0 u
21		21 1 0 u
22		22 1 0 u
23		23 1 0 u
24		24 1 0 u

Part 4

		Do not write below here
25		25 2 1 0 u
26		26 2 1 0 u
27		27 2 1 0 u
28		28 2 1 0 u
29		29 2 1 0 u
30		30 2 1 0 u

Part 5

31	A	B	C	D
32	A	B	C	D
33	A	B	C	D
34	A	B	C	D
35	A	B	C	D
36	A	B	C	D

Part 6

37	A	B	C	D	E	F	G
38	A	B	C	D	E	F	G
39	A	B	C	D	E	F	G
40	A	B	C	D	E	F	G
41	A	B	C	D	E	F	G
42	A	B	C	D	E	F	G

Part 7

43	A	B	C	D	E	F
44	A	B	C	D	E	F
45	A	B	C	D	E	F
46	A	B	C	D	E	F
47	A	B	C	D	E	F
48	A	B	C	D	E	F
49	A	B	C	D	E	F
50	A	B	C	D	E	F
51	A	B	C	D	E	F
52	A	B	C	D	E	F

CAMBRIDGE ENGLISH
Language Assessment
Part of the University of Cambridge

Do not write in this box

S A M P L E

Candidate Name
If not already printed, write name in CAPITALS and complete the Candidate No. grid (in pencil).

Candidate Signature

Examination Title

Centre

Supervisor:
If the candidate is ABSENT or has WITHDRAWN shade here

Centre No.

Candidate No.

Examination Details

0	0	0	0
1	1	1	1
2	2	2	2
3	3	3	3
4	4	4	4
5	5	5	5
6	6	6	6
7	7	7	7
8	8	8	8
9	9	9	9

Candidate Answer Sheet

Instructions

Use a PENCIL (B or HB).
Rub out any answer you wish to change using an eraser.

Parts 1, 3 and **4:**
Mark ONE letter for each question.

For example, if you think **B** is the right answer to the question, mark your answer sheet like this:

0 A B C

Part 2:
Write your answer clearly in CAPITAL LETTERS.

Write one letter or number in each box.
If the answer has more than one word, leave one box empty between words.

For example:

0 AN EXAMPLE

Turn this sheet over to start.

Part 1

1	A	B	C
2	A	B	C
3	A	B	C
4	A	B	C
5	A	B	C
6	A	B	C
7	A	B	C
8	A	B	C

Part 2 (Remember to write in CAPITAL LETTERS or numbers)

Do not write below here

9		9 1 0 u
10		10 1 0 u
11		11 1 0 u
12		12 1 0 u
13		13 1 0 u
14		14 1 0 u
15		15 1 0 u
16		16 1 0 u
17		17 1 0 u
18		18 1 0 u

Part 3

19	A	B	C	D	E	F	G	H
20	A	B	C	D	E	F	G	H
21	A	B	C	D	E	F	G	H
22	A	B	C	D	E	F	G	H
23	A	B	C	D	E	F	G	H

Part 4

24	A	B	C
25	A	B	C
26	A	B	C
27	A	B	C
28	A	B	C
29	A	B	C
30	A	B	C

Acknowledgements

The authors and publishers acknowledge the following sources of copyright material and are grateful for the permissions granted. While every effort has been made, it has not always been possible to identify the sources of all the material used, or to trace all copyright holders. If any omissions are brought to our notice, we will be happy to include the appropriate acknowledgements on reprinting and in the next update to the digital edition, as applicable.

Key: B = Below, T = Top.

Text

Dogo Media Inc. for the text on p. 10 adapted from 'Scientists Confirm That In Order To Succeed, You Have To First Fail' by Avery Elizabeth Hurt, 09.12.2014. Copyright © 2014 Dogo Media Inc. Reproduced with permission; Guardian News & Media Ltd. for the text on p. 14 adapted from 'An author at 15: teenage girls had to be ugly, naive or antisocial' by Kate Kellaway, *The Guardian*, 01.02.2015. Copyright © 2015 Guardian News & Media Ltd. Reproduced with permission; Guardian News & Media Ltd. for the text on adapted p. 16 from 'Swedish school sheds light on dark days on winter' by David Crouch, *The Guardian*, 24.01.2015. Copyright © 2015 Guardian News & Media Ltd. Reproduced with permission; New York Daily News for the text on p.33 adapted from "New Yorkers encouraged to 'act like a kid' and jump on bed in middle of city" by Joel Landau, Daily News, 02.12.2014. Copyright © 2014 New York Daily News. Reproduced with permission; Los Angeles Times for the text on p. 36 from 'Teens Launch Balloons To Edge Of Space, And So The Adventure Begins' by Deborah Netburn, Los Angeles Times, 17.06.2014. Copyright © 2014 Los Angeles Times. Reproduced with permission; Dogo Media Inc. for the text on p. 38 adapted from 'Crafty Seals Seek Follow Tracking Device Signals To Catch Fish' by Meera Dolasla, 20.11.2014. Copyright © 2014 Dogo Media Inc. Reproduced with permission; The Washington Post for the text on p. 60 from 'Scientists have discovered a new taste that could profoundly change the way we meet' by Roberto A. Ferdman, *The Washington Post*. Copyright © 2017 The Washington Post. Reproduced with permission; NBCUniversal Archives for the text on p. 80 from 'Family road trips: Getting there is not half the fun' by Eric Ruhlater, 15.11.2012. Copyright © 2012 NBCUniversal Archives. Reproduced with permission; Dogo Media Inc. for the text on p. 136 adapted from 'Scientists Discover Spectacular Ruby-Red Seadragon' by Allegra Staples, 26.02.2015. Copyright © 2015 Dogo Media Inc. Reproduced with permission.

Photos

All photographs are sourced from Getty Images.

p. C1 (T): Hill Street Studios/Blend Images; p. C1 (B), p. C5 (B), p. C10 (T): Hero Images; p. C2 (T): Sean De Burca/The Image Bank; p. C2 (B), p. C4 (T): Steve Debenport/E+; p. C4 (B), p. C7 (T): asiseeit/E+; p. C5 (T): Sam Edwards/Caiaimage; p. C7 (B): Robert Daly/Caiaimage; p. C8 (T): Emir Memedovski/E+; p. C8 (B): MivPiv/ E+; p. C10 (B): Hero Images/DigitalVision; p. C11 (T): Christa Paustenbaugh Photography/Moment Open; p. C11 (B): PeopleImages/E+.

Visual materials for the Speaking test

What are the people enjoying about doing these activities in after school clubs?

1A

1B

Why have the people decided to take photographs in these situations?

1C

1D

1E

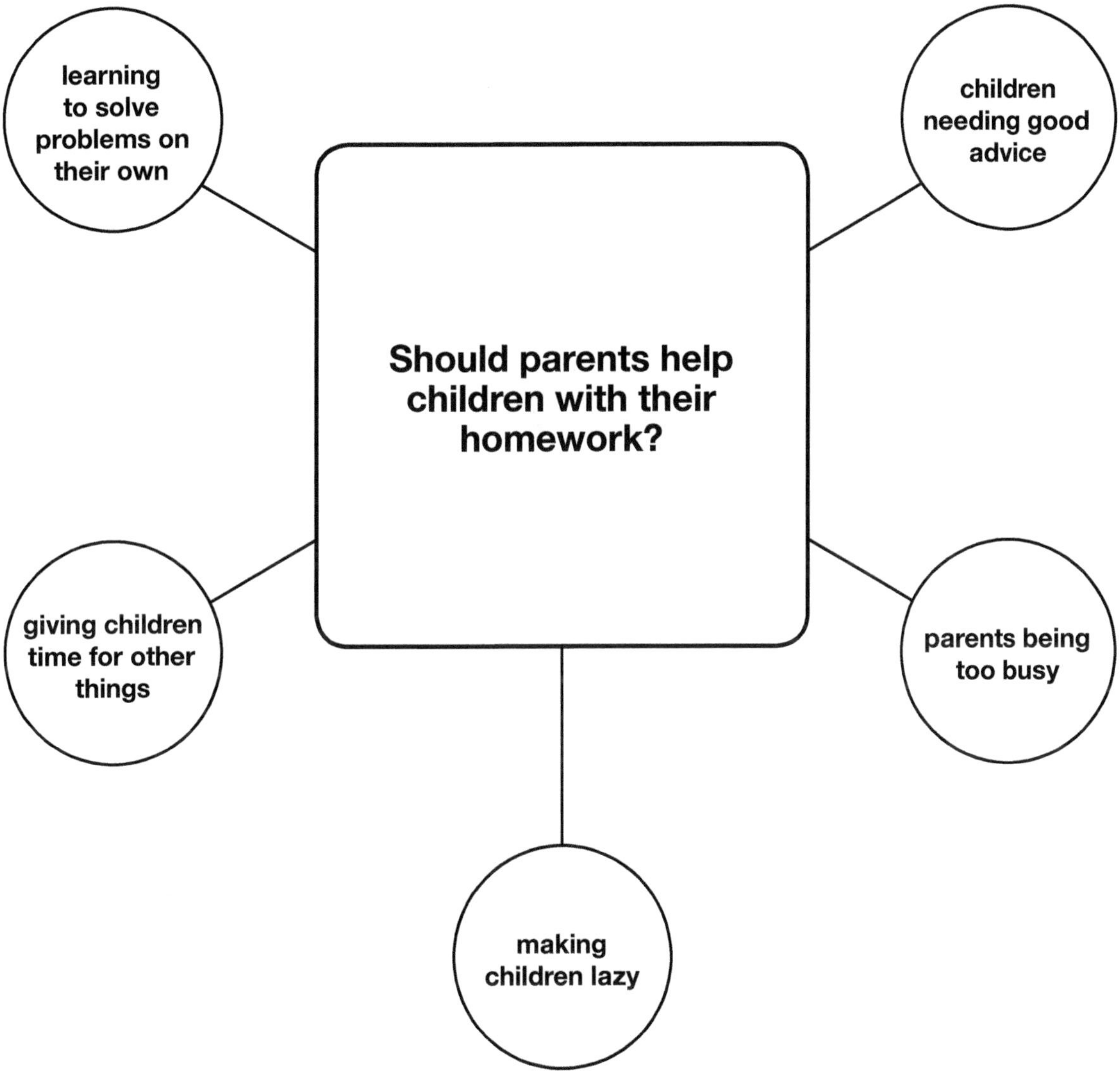
Should parents help children with their homework?
learning to solve problems on their own
children needing good advice
giving children time for other things
parents being too busy
making children lazy

Why are the people listening carefully in these situations?

2A

2B

What are the families enjoying about spending their holidays in these places?

2C

2D

2E

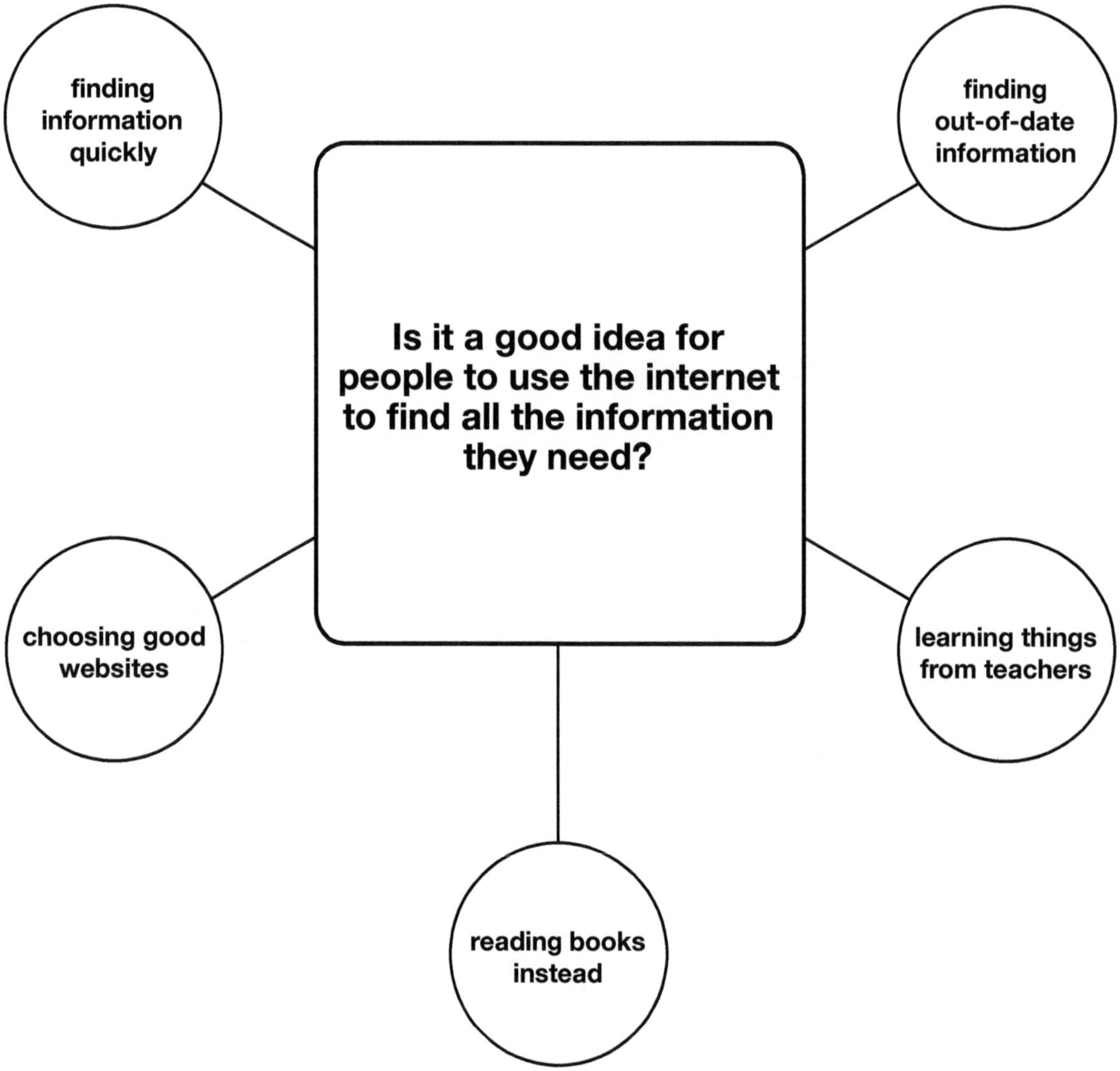
Is it a good idea for people to use the internet to find all the information they need?
finding information quickly
finding out-of-date information
choosing good websites
learning things from teachers
reading books instead

Why are the people working together in these situations?

3A

3B

What is difficult for the people about learning these things?

3C

3D

3E

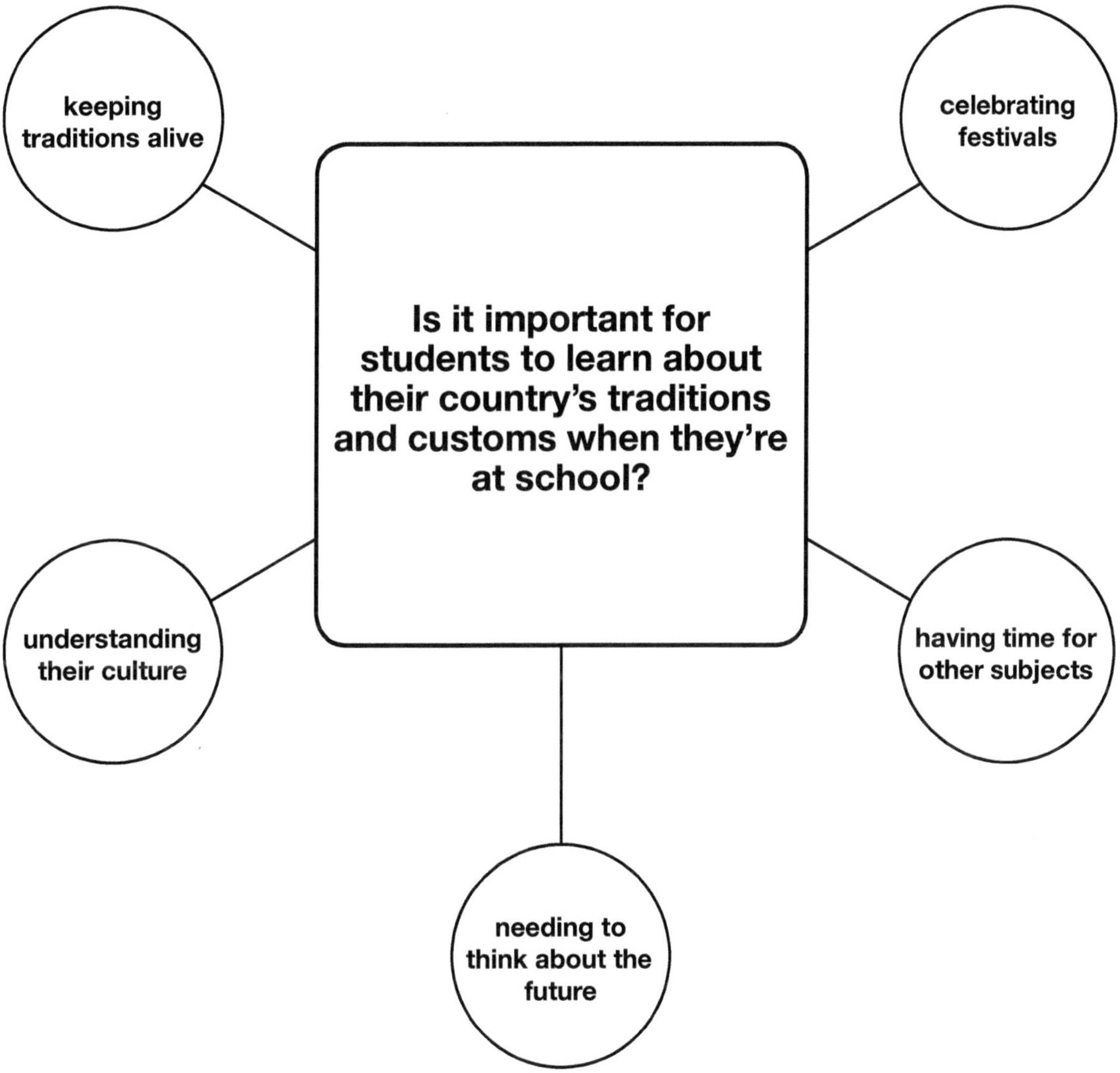
Is it important for students to learn about their country's traditions and customs when they're at school?
keeping traditions alive
celebrating festivals
understanding their culture
having time for other subjects
needing to think about the future

What are the advantages of studying science in these ways?

4A

4B

Why have these people decided to spend time on their own?

4C

4D

4E

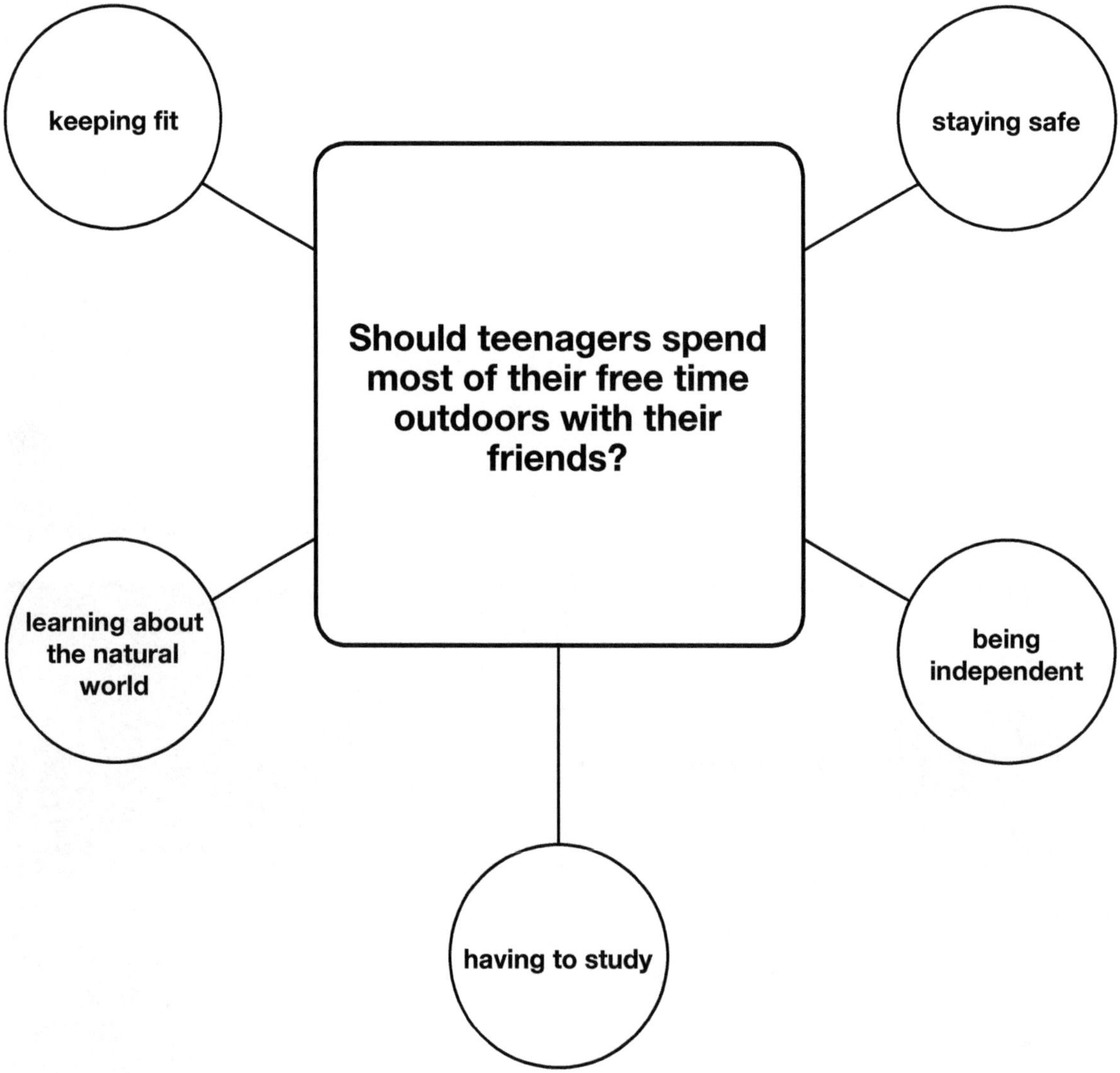
Should teenagers spend most of their free time outdoors with their friends?
keeping fit
staying safe
learning about the natural world
being independent
having to study